GEOGRAPHY OF MARKETING AND COMMERCIAL ACTIVITIES IN INDIA

CONCEPTS IN COMMUNICATION INFORMATICS & LIBRARIANSHIP (CICIL)

General Editor: **S.P. AGRAWAL**

CICIL-1	Development of Library Services in India: Social Science Information **S.P. Agrawal**	Rs. 150 $ 30
CICIL-2	Development of Documentation in India: Social Science Information **S.P. Agrawal**	Rs. 250 $ 50
CICIL-3	UNESCO and Social Sciences: Retrospect and Prospect **S.P. Agrawal** and **J.C. Aggarwal**	Rs. 250 $ 50
CICIL-4	INDIANA: A Bibliography of Bibliographical Sources **M.K. Jain**	Rs. 200 $ 40
CICIL-5	Dimensions of Library and Information Science: Papers contributed in honour of the 61st birthday celebrations of Prof. P.N. Kaula **V. Venkatappaiah** (Ed.)	(in press)
CICIL-6	Book Numbers: Some Indian Methods **M.P. Satija** and **S.P. Agrawal**	(in press)
CICIL-7	National Policy for University Libraries in India: Problems and Perspectives **N.B. Inamdar** and **L.S. Ramaiah** (Ed.)	Rs. 250 $ 50
CICIL-8	Media Utilisation for the Development of Women and Children **B.S. Thakur** and **Binod C. Agrawal**	Rs. 150 $ 30
CICIL-9	Terrorism: An Annotated Bibliography **Susheela Bhan**	Rs. 300 $ 60
CICIL-10	Transnational Library Relations: The Indo-American Experience **M.B. Konnur**	(in press)
CICIL-11	Geography of Marketing and Commercial Activities in India (Documentation on Research Information) **R.S. Dixit**	Rs. 130 $ 26
CICIL-12	Information India 1988: Global View **S.P. Agrawal** and **J.C. Aggarwal**	Rs. 200 $ 40

Concepts in Communication
Informatics & Librarianship-11

General Editor: **S.P. Agrawal**

Geography of Marketing and Commercial Activities in India

Documentation on Research Information

R.S. DIXIT

Foreword by
Prof. **R.P. MISRA**

CONCEPT PUBLISHING COMPANY, NEW DELHI-110059

The Government of Uttar Pradesh adjudged this work as "an outstanding one" and also awarded.

ISBN 81-7022-272-9

First Published 1990

Ram Swaroop **Dixit** (*b*. 1941)

Published by
Ashok Kumar Mittal
Concept Publishing Company
A/15-16, Commercial Block, Mohan Garden
NEW DELHI-110059 (India)

Lasertypeset by
Microtech Advance Printing Systems (Pvt.) Ltd.
H-13 Bali Nagar,
NEW DELHI-110015

Printed in India by:
D.B. Offset Works
New Delhi-110028

DEDICATED

TO

MY INSPIRATION, MY BELOVED WIFE

ASHA DIXIT

Foreword

SPATIAL ASPECTS of marketing have not received adequate attention by Indian geographers. It is only recently that a few of them have done considerable work deserving professional attention and recognition. This new situation has encouraged a number of young geographers to take Marketing Geography as a specialized field of study.

Marketing consists of almost all the processes – purchase, sale, transportation, storage, aspects of processing, costing, pricing, planning, etc. which carry a given commodity from the source of production to the ultimate consumer. All these can be seen from a variety of perspectives. Geographers view marketing from spatial angle giving importance to market centres, movement of goods and services, market areas, impact of space on prices and costs and marketing and development. Recent works on spatial allocation model have opened up new areas of research and action.

Conventional work on market centres using Christaller's central place theory became quite common in India during the '50s and '60s. Other aspects remained practically neglected. As regards education and training, no department of geography in the country specialized in Market Geography until early '70s when the Institute of Development Studies, University of Mysore (then a research wing of the Department of Post-Graduate Studies and Research in Geography) launched a major project on Agricultural Marketing. This project consisted of two main activities: (1) Post-Graduate degree programme in Agricultural Marketing Management and (2) Research on the functioning and development of regulated markets in Karnataka.

Since then a number of seminars and conferences have been held under the auspices of geography departments and a number of books have been brought out giving the proceedings of these meetings and results of research work. A few persons among the host geographers interested in marketing geography stand out prominently - Dr. R.S. Dixit, University of Lucknow, Prof. D.C. Jayasankar, University of Mysore, and Dr. V.K. Shrivastava, University of Gorakhpur.

I have been fortunate to have known all these scholars from close quarters. I have seen them moving up haltingly to begin with; and then trying not only to break new grounds through their personal researches but also helping others to take up new research challenges in the field. I am, therefore, glad indeed to see Dr. Dixit bring out the present volume - *Geography of Marketing and Commercial Activities in India: Documentation on Research Information.*

Dr. Dixit has taken lot of pains to bring out this volume which I am sure will be of immense help to market researchers. Research literature documented in this volume has been classified in a number of ways for easy identification. Moreover, the latest material finds a place in the volume making it a highly valuable book.

Dr. Dixit deserves all the appreciation for this contribution. I am confident that the volume will be of considerable use to the students of Marketing Geography and allied disciplines.

Delhi
1st May, 1989

R.P. MISRA

General Editor's Introduction

CICIL IS a new series launched by the publishers covering communication, information technology and librarianship fields which are interrelated and which, at the same time, in themselves include in their scope a very wide strech of topics for investigation, research and study.

Communication is a quality of the sentient. Homosapiens, high up in the evolutionary order, had fashioned many modes and mediums of expression. Of late, technology has armed man with dynamic and effective communication. All this necessitates us to reflect on the role of librarian in the emerging scenario. Librarianship, the grand discipline with the art and science of management, in a sense lords over all the subjects. The present series will look at ideas, old and new, in all the allied areas.

With the advance of knowledge, based on research, new avenues are opened to scholars. Marketing Geography, in this context, is one such branch, which has been developed of late, and it has since become the corner-stone of all commercial activities.

The Chapters that follow in this publication offer a scientific treatment to the various aspects of marketing geography. Out of the 13 Chapters on the subject, the first deals with the method of presentation, while the second gives reviews and bibliographies on literature, keeping the world context in one's mind.

A rich inventory in the Indian perspective gives details of research books and monographs, research project reports, research articles and a classified data base of research contributions and an exhaustive bibliography.

S. P. AGRAWAL

Contents

List of Tables

Preface

MARKETING GEOGRAPHY has come up as a distinct sub-field of geography both in the developed and the developing nations. Within the International Geographical Union, the specific units – Working Group (1972-1984) and Study Group (1984 onwards), had been formed to promote research activities in this area of study. In India, too, this sub-field has achieved the status of a branch of the discipline of geography. The geography scholars in the country have shown keen interest in undertaking the studies on various perspectives of marketing in India and it is a good sign that the number of researchers and researches has been constantly increasing during the past years. In several Indian universities, Marketing Geography has been included in the syllabus of Post-Graduate studies as a special paper. However, there is a characteristic absence of a work which could guide the scholars for further work by (i) presenting the stock of existing literature as well as (ii) pointing out the perspectives of the potential/future studies. The objective of the endeavour, one in hand, primarily is to meet the necessary requirement in this very direction. The project on which the present report is based was funded by the Indian Council of Social Science Research, New Delhi. However, the responsibility for the facts stated, opinions expressed and conclusions reached is entirely that of the project director and not of the Indian Council of Social Science Research.

I gratefully acknowledge the blessings extended to me by Professor R.P. Misra, Head of the Geography Department (Delhi University), and the help from Dr. D.N. Verma and Dr. R.B. Chaturvedi (Avadh University) in transforming my mental picturesque into a concrete reality. I like to express my sincere thanks to Shri D.P. Gupta for completing the typing work of the manuscript within a very short period of time.

Last, but not the least, I wish to express my heartfelt gratitude to my inspiration, my beloved wife Asha Dixit, who, in fact, aroused my interest in the making of this research monograph on inventory and prospects of the marketing perspectives in the context of India. The work, really, would not have come into being without the continued inspiration and encouragement from Ashaji.

Hope, the monograph would fill up the most-felt void in the studies in geography of marketing and commercial activities in the country.

R.S. DIXIT

SECTION A
PROLOGUE

1

INTRODUCTION

MARKETING activity is as old as human society itself. Barter system was a common practice among the people in early days of civilization. With the passage of time and development of civilization, the tertiary activities also became more complex and complicated. Such activities have attracted the attention of social scientists for indepth studies, especially, in the second-half of the present century.

Marketing geography is one of the recently developed sub-fields of the geographical sciences. In the western world, the offshoot of marketing geography was first identified by William Applebaum during the early 1950s. During the early 1960s, R.E. Murphy laid great emphasis on the fact that marketing geography had come of age. Credit goes to R.J. Bromley (1971, 1974a, b, 1979) for presenting several lists of literature on marketing geography in the form of review and bibliographies during the 1970s. With the establishment of the International Geographical Union Working Group on Market Distribution System/Market Place Exchange Systems (1972-1973, Co-chairmen: E. Gormsen and R.H.T. Smith), the formative process of marketing geography rapidly started taking place. R.H.T. Smith (1979, 1980) contributed to this sub-field by presenting two very significant papers on 'review and prospect'. In 1985, E. Gormsen edited the 15th Newsletter of the Working Group in which he included the bibliography compiled by Wayne McKim in this area of geography. After the termination of the term of the Working Group on Market Place Exchange Systems (1984), a new unit 'Study Group: Geography of Commercial Activities' had come into being to continue the research activities as per approval of the General Conference of the International Geographical Union held in Paris (1984). Later, this group converted into Commission (1988).

Unfortunately, no bibliography or any kind of inventory of Geography of Marketing/Commercial Activities has come into existence in India in the form of a monograph till the date. The objective of this attempt, primarily, is to present an exhaustive inventory of the literature in this sub-field of geography in the country. Further, the attempt has been supplemented with a discussion on various prospective perspectives too.

The design of the work comprises three sections: A, B, and C. The details of the design are as follows:

SECTION A: PROLOGUE

1. Introduction
2. Reviews and Bibliographies on Literature -The World Context

SECTION B: INVENTORY -THE INDIAN CONTEXT

3. Reviews and Bibliographies on Literature
4. Research Books and Monographs - I
5. Research Books and Monographs - II
6. Research Project Reports - I
7. Research Project Reports - II
8. (i) Research Articles - I
   (ii) Research Articles - I
9. Research Articles - II
10. Research Contributions - Classified
11. Bibliography

SECTION C: EPILOGUE

12. Overview of the Project
13. Prospective Perspectives

REVIEWS AND BIBLIOGRAPHIES ON LITERATURE – THE WORLD CONTEXT

This part of the work has been devoted to highlight the notable works on reviews, references, inventories, and bibliographies on the literature on geography of marketing/commercial activities in the world context.

William Applebaum is widely regarded as the chief architect of marketing geography as a distinct field of study in the United States. He wrote a section on 'Marketing Geography' in the volume, *American Geography - Inventory and Prospects* (eds: James, P.E. and Jones, C.F., 1954). In 1955 Applebaum, W. and Selapken, B.L. brought out an 'Atlas of Business Centres'. Besides, Applebaum contributed to the sub-field of marketing geography by presenting a number of research papers on varied perspectives.

In view of a good number of research papers and the keen interest shown by geographers in marketing geography, R.E. Murphy (1961) was inspired to present a write-up entitled 'Marketing geography comes of age' in a volume of *Economic Geography* (37) in early 1960s.

During the 1970s R.J. Bromley made valuable contributions to this sub-field of geography by presenting his works on review (1971) and bibliographies (1974 a, b; 1979) on the literature of marketing geography.

Two papers on review and prospect were contributed by R.H.T. Smith (1979, 1980) in 'Progress in Human Geography', 3(4), 4(1) in which he included long lists of contributions under 'references'.

Thus, on reviews, references, inventories, and bibliographies, the above mentioned nine works (Table 1) have proved to be notable and these works have led the scholars in the sub-field of marketing geography for further research work.

TABLE 1: REVIEWS AND BIBLIOGRAPHIES — THE WORLD CONTEXT

Decade/Year		*Researcher*	*Theme: major class*
1950s:			
	1954:	Applebaum, W.	Marketing Geography: Inventory
	1955:	Applebaum, W. & Selapken, B.L.	Atlas on Business Centres: Inventory
1960s:			
	1961:	Murphy, R.E.	Marketing Geography: Comes of Age
1970s:			
	1971:	Bromley, R.J.	Markets in Developing Countries: Review
	1974(a):	Bromley, R.J.	Market Place Studies: Bibliography
	1974(b):	Bromley, R.J.	Periodic Markets, Daily Markets and Fairs: Bibliography
	1979:	Bromley, R.J.	Periodic Markets, Daily Markets and Fairs: Bibliography (supplement to 1974b)
	1979:	Smith, R.H.T.	Periodic Market Places: Review and Prospect
1980s:			
	1980:	Smith, R.H.T.	Periodic Market Places: Review and Prospect

REVIEWS, REFERENCES, AND BIBLIOGRAPHIES ON LITERATURE

Section B has been divided into nine parts and all the perspectives relate to the works on various aspects arranged in chronological order as well as alphabetical order presenting a vivid picture of inventory of literature on marketing geography in the country.

This part of the section is one of the above mentioned parts and presents an inventory of the reviews, references, and bibliographies on the literature. The inventory unfolds these sources which are as many as twenty five in number. Table 2 demonstrates the work related to inventory of literature in geography of marketing and commercial activities.

TABLE 2: REVIEWS, REFERENCES, AND BIBLIOGRAPHIES ON LITERATURE — THE INDIAN CONTEXT

Sl. No.	*Decade/Year*	*Scholar (Chronological Order)*	*Scholar (Alphabetical Order)*	*Year*
	1970s:			
1.	1972*	Shafi, M.	Arunachalam, B.	: 1983+
2.	1977	Saxena, H.N.	Concept Pub. Co.	: 1982
3.	1979*	Singh, J.	Dixit, R.S.	: 1984(a), 1984(b), 1986
	1980s:			
4.	1980	Saxena, H.N.		
5.	1980	Sami, A.		
6.	1980	Singh, L.R.		
7.	1980	Dixit, R.S. and Verma, D.N.	Dixit, R.S. and Verma, D.N.	: 1980
8.	1982	Concept Pub. Co.	Gormsen, E.	: 1985
9.	1983+	Arunachalam, B.	ICSSR	: Undated (Also 1972,1979,1984)
10.	1983	Sinha, B.N.		
11.	1984	Tiwari, R.C. and Tripathi, S.		
12.	1984	Sinha, B.N.	Ishihara, H.	: 1985
13.	1984*	Jayashankar, D.C.	Jayashankar, D.C.	: 1984*
14.	1984a	Dixit, R.S.		
15.	1984b	Dixit, R.S.	Metton, A.	: 1986 a, b; 1987
16.	1984	Srivastava, V.K.	Sami, A.	: 1980
17.	1985+	Srivastava, V.K.		
18.	1985	Gormsen, E.	Saxena, H.M.	: 1977, 1980
19.	1985	Ishihara, H.	Shafi, M.	: 1972*
20.	1986	Sinha, B.N.		
21.	1986	Dixit, R.S.	Singh, J.	: 1979*
22.	1986a	Metton, A.	Singh, L.R.	: 1980
23.	1986b	Metton, A.	Singh, L.R.	: 1980
24.	1987	Metton, A.		
25.	Undated	ICSSR	Sinha, B.N.	: 1983, 1984, 1986
			Srivastava, V.K.	: 1984, 1985+
			Tiwari, R.C. and Tripathi, S.	: 1984

+ Shows unpublished paper;
* For ICSSR

NOTABLE BOOKS BY INDIAN SCHOLARS

The chronological list of notable books in marketing geography shows that there are nearly three and a half dozens of works which are worth mention. Table 3 illustrates that with the passage of time the researchers in this area of study increased in considerable number, especially, during the 1970s and 1980s.

TABLE 3: CONTRIBUTORS OF NOTABLE BOOKS: INDIAN SCHOLARS

Sl. No.	*Decade/Year*	*Author*	*Sl. No.*	*Decade/Year*	*Author*
1.	1930s: 1930	Pant, D.	22.	1979	Dixit, R.S.
2.	1937	Hussain, S.A.	23.	1979	Raza, M. (For ICSSR)
3.	1950s: 1951	Kulkarni and Karwe, I.			
4.	1953	Mitra, A.	24.	1980s: 1980	Sami, A.
5.	1956	Baranu,H. and Baneja, J.D.	25.	1980	Wanmali, S.
6.	1960s: 1965(a)	NCAER	26.	1982	Concept Pub Co.
7.	1965(b)	NCAER	27.	1982	Ramachandran, H.
8.	1968	Sinha, D.P.	28.	1983	Sinha, B.N.
9.	1970s: 1971	Rao, B.P.	29.	1984	Sinha, B.N.
10.	1972	ICSSR	30.	1986	Sinha, B.N.
11.	1972	NCAER	31.	1980	ICSSR
12.	1974	Sinha, B.N.	32.	1981	ICSSR
13.	1975	ICSSR	33.	1982	ICSSR
14.	1976	ICSSR	34.	1984	ICSSR
15.	1977	ICSSR	35.	1984	Saxena, H.M.
16.	1978	ICSSR	36.	1983	Srivastava, V.K.
17.	1979	ICSSR	37.	1984	Srivastava, V.K.
18.	1975	Chaudhry, S.	38.	1987	Srivastava, V.K.
19.	1975	Saxena, H.M.	39.	1984	Dixit, R.S.
20.	1978	Pal, M.K.	40.	1985	ICRISAT*
21.	1979	Leon, S.	41.	Undated India	

Contributor		*Contribution*
ICSSR	: 11	(1972, 1979, 1984; 1975, 1976, 1977, 1978, 1979, 1980, 1981, 1982)
NCAER	: 3	(1965, 1965, 1972)
Sinha, B.N.	: 3	(1983, 1984, 1986)
Srivastava, V.K.	: 3	(1983, 1984, 1987)
Saxena, H.M.	: 2	(1975, 1984)
Dixit, R.S.	: 2	(1979, 1984)
ICRISAT	: 1	(1985)
Concept Pub Co.	: 1	(1982)
Others One Each	: 15	

* International Crop Research Institute for the Semi_Arid Tropics, Patancheru, Hyderabad.

NOTABLE BOOKS: OTHERS ON INDIAN PERSPECTIVES

Some other researchers also have worked on the issues related to marketing aspects of various parts of India. Nearly two and a half dozens of such works have been traced by the author through various sources. Most of these books appeared after the 1960s (and more specifically during the 1980s). H. Ishihara (1961, 1978, 1979, 1983ab, 1985ab) and B. Harriss have shown keen interest in undertaking various projects/schemes related to market place systems, especially, of south India. Table 4 shows the relevant details of these books.

TABLE 4: CONTRIBUTORS OF NOTABLE BOOKS: OTHERS ON INDIAN PERSPECTIVES

Sl. No.	*Decade/Year*		*Author*	*Sl. No.*	*Decade/Year*	*Author*
1.	1920s:	1929	Bentley, O.A.	15.	1983(a)	Ishihara, H.
2.	1960s:	1961	Ishihara, H.	16.	1983(b)	Ishihara, H.
3-9.	1970s:	1973-1979	IGU Working Group, Newsletters 7 Nos.	17.	1985(a)	Ishihara, H.
				18.	1985(b)	Ishihara, H.
10.		1978	Ishihara, H	19.-26.	1980-1985	IGU Working Group Newsletters 8 Nos.
11.		1979	Ishihara, H.			
12.	1980s:	1981(a)	Harriss, B..	27.-29.	1986-1987	IGU Study Group Newsletters 3 Nos.
13.		1984(a)	Harriss, B.			
14.		1984(b)	Harriss, B.			

Contributor		*Contribution*
Ishihara, H.	: 7	1961, 1978, 1979, 1983a, 1983b, 1985a, 1985b
Harriss, B.	: 3	1981a, 1984a, 1984b
Bentley, O.A.	: 1	1929
IGU Working Group	: 15	Newsletters from 1973 - 1985
IGU Study Group	: 3	Newsletters from 1986 - 1987

DISSERTATIONS BY INDIAN SCHOLARS

The chronological list of dissertations shows that a good number of scholars have completed their dissertations leading to various degrees, mostly doctoral, in the country. Nearly two and a half dozens of dissertations have been completed in various universities, about one and a half dozens in number, on perspectives relating to marketing within the sphere of geography. To be exact, there are two M.Phil., one M.A., one M.C.P., and twenty-five Ph.D. dissertations in the list known to the author (Table 5).

Also, the research contributions in this direction, although, started from the 1950s but most of the contributions belong to the 1970s and 1980s.

TABLE 5: DISSERTATIONS BY INDIAN SCHOLARS

Sl. No.	*Decade/Year*		*Scholar*
1.	**1950s:**	1958	Singh, S.M. (M.A.), B.H.U.
2.		1959	Rao, R. (D. Phil), Allahabad University
3.	**1960s:**	1962	Singh, K.N. (Ph.D.), B.H.U.
4.		1964	Barnum, H. (Ph.D.), Berkley
5.		1964	Sinha, D.P. (Ph.D.), South Illinois
6.		1966	Vishwanath, M.S. (Ph.D.), B.H.U.
7.		1968	Sinha, M.K. (M.C.P.), I.I.T., Kharagpur
8.	**1970s:**	1971	Saxena, H.M. (Ph.D.), Udaipur University
9.		1973	Kumavat, B.L. (Ph.D.), Udaipur University
10.		1975	Sami, A. (Ph.D.), Patna University
11.		1976	Nolakha, R.L. (Ph.D.), Rajasthan University
12.		1977	Geetha, T. (M.Phil.), Madras University
13.		1977	Swaminathan, E. (Ph.D.), Madras University
14.		1978	Chandran, K. (M.Phil.), Madurai University
15.		1978	Gedam, D.A. (Ph.D.), Nagpur University
16.		1978	Parvathi, C. (Ph.D.), Mysore University
17.		1978	Wanmali, S. (Ph.D.), Cambridge University
18.		1979	Maidamwar, G.T. (Ph.D.), Nagpur University
19.		1979	Rathore, N.S. (Ph.D.), Udaipur University
20.		1979	Vishwanath, V.V, (Ph.D.), Madras University
21.		1979	Dixit, R.S. (D.Phil.), Allahabad University
22.	**1980s:**	1980	Mohanty, S.K. (Ph.D.), Utkal University
23.		1980	Srivastava, H.O. (Ph.D.), Gorakhpur University
24.		1982	Ram, U. (Ph.D.), Gorakhpur University
25.		1983	Nath, V. (Ph.D.), Gorakhpur University
26.		1983	Sharma, P.K. (Ph.D.), Utkal University
27.		1983	Srivastava, K.R. (Ph.D.), Jabalpur University
28.		1984	Hugar, S.I. (Ph.D.), Dharwad University
29.		1987	Verma, R.D. (Ph.D.), Kanpur university

University	Number of Dissertations	Scholar/Year
Allahabad	2	Dixit, R.S., 1979; Rao, R., 1959
B.H.U.	3	Singh, S.M., 1958; Singh, K.N., 1962; Vishwanath, M.S., 1966
Bhubaneshwar	2	Mohanty, S.K., 1980; Sharma, P.K., 1983
Berkley	1	Barnum, H., 1964
Cambridge	1	Wanmali, S., 1978
Dharwad	1	Hugar, S.I., 1984
Gorakhpur	3	Srivastava, H.O., 1980; Ram, U., 1982; Nath, V., 1983
Illinois	1	Sinha, D.P., 1964
Jabalpur	1	Srivastava, K.R., 1983
Kanpur	1	Verma, R.D., 1987
Kharagpur	1	Sinha, M.K., 1968
Madras	3	Geetha, T., 1977; Vishwanath, V.V., 1979; Swaminathan, E., 1976
Madurai	1	Chandran, K., 1978
Mysore	1	Parvathi, C., 1978
Nagpur	2	Gedam, D.A., 1978; Maidamwar, G.T., 1979
Patna	1	Sami, A., 1975
Rajasthan	1	Nolakha, R.L., 1976
Udaipur	3	Saxena, H.M., 1971; Kumawat, B.L., 1973; Rathore, N.S., 1979
	29	

RESEARCH PROJECT REPORTS BY INDIAN SCHOLARS

Indian scholars have shown keen interest in taking up various research projects, mostly post-doctoral level, sponsored by the research institutes/departments of the governmental/non-governmental agencies in the country. Some significant details of these projects have been provided in Table 6. It is clear from the table that at least a dozen projects have been completed by the Indian scholars in the geography of marketing/commercial activities.

RESEARCH ARTICLES BY INDIAN SCHOLARS

Following an archival research, the author has come across 398 research articles, that is, published papers, published abstracts, and unpublished papers contributed to the sub-field of geography of marketing/commercial activities by the Indian scholars.

TABLE 6: RESEARCH PROJECT REPORTS BY INDIAN SCHOLARS

Sl. No.	*Decade/Year*		*Scholar*	*Sponsoring Department/Institute, etc.*
1.	**1960s:**	1961	Prakash Rao, V.L.S.	Ministry of Health, New Delhi
2.		1967	Khan, W.	Metropolitan Research, Hyderabad
3.	**1970s:**	1970	Karwe, I. and Acharya, H.	ICSSR, New Delhi
4.		1971	Joshi, V.K.	S.P. University
5.		1979	Tamaskar, B.G.	U.G.C., New Delhi
6.	**1980s:**	1980	Saxena, H.M.	ICSSR, New Delhi
7.		1980	Patil, S.P. and Pawat, J.R.	Mahatona Phule Krishi, Bombay
8.		1980	Raju, V.T. and Oppen, von M.	ICRISAT, Hyderabad
9.		1982	Raju, V.T. and Oppen, von M.	ICRISAT, Hyderabad
10.		1982	Srivastava, V.K.	ICSSR, New Delhi
11.		1983	Wanmali, S.	IFRI, Washington D.C.
12.		1984	Dixit, R.S.	ICSSR, New Delhi

The inventory has been developed in the form of typologies based on sub-themes of the research articles arranged in two ways:

The first typology presents a chronological panorama of articles under 16 different perspectives of market studies, viz., Role, Origin/Evolution, Location/Distribution, Transport Network, Typology, Centrality/Hierarchy, Trade Area, Structure/Morphology, Consumer/Trader Behaviour, Synchronization/Rings or Cycles, Traditional Exchange/Periodic Marketing, Urban or Daily/Agri-cultural or Regulated Markets, Function, Goods/Commodities, Planning, and Others.

The second typology, on the other hand, reveals the contributions arranged in alphabetical order by the same researchers under the same 16 sub-heads. It is important to note that most of the articles have appeared during the 1970s and 1980s. Table 7(i) and 7(ii) illustrate all the relevant particulars of the same.

TABLE 7(i): THEMATIC TYPOLOGY OF RESEARCH ARTICLES BY INDIAN SCHOLARS (I)

Decade	*No. of Articles*	*No. of Perspectives*	*Number of Articles Under Various Perspectives*															
			1	2	3	4	5	6	7	8	9	10	11	12	13	14	15	16
1930s	8	5			4				3				3			5		2
1940s	8	7			5				3				5	2	1	5		1
1950s	8	(		2	4				4				5			4		3
1960s	33	15	9	14	23	6	3	1	19	3	3		9	6	8	13	2	5
1970s	127	16	24	33	47	10	8	15	25	20	10	7	35	32	18	15	37	45
1980s	214	16	45	36	59	19	28	25	27	18	30	36	79	53	16	24	32	70
Total	398	16	78	85	142	35	39	41	81	41	43	43	136	93	43	66	71	126

Year-wise Break-ups of Number of Articles during the 1960s, 1970s, 1980s.

1960s	*1970s*	*1980s*
1960 - 1	1970 - 1	1980 -33
1961 - 3	1971 - 1+1	1981 -19
1962 - 1	1972 - 44	1982 -19
1963 - 8	1973 - 4	1983 -40
1965 - 4	1974 - 11	1984 -28
1966 - 5	1975 - 10	1985 -58
1967 - 3	1976 - 12	1986 -11
1968 - 5	1977 - 11	1987 - 6
1969 - 3	1978 - 12	
	1979 -14+3	
33	127	214

TABLE 7(II): THEMATIC TYPOLOGY OF RESEARCH ARTICLES BY INDIAN SCHOLARS (II)

Sl. No.	Perspective	Number of Contributions	Researcher (Number of Contributions)
1.	Role	78	DRS(11), SVK(3), TBG(2), VSC(2), WS(2), NCAER(2), India(9) = 31 contributions + 47 others (1 each)
2.	Origin/Evolution	85	DRS(10), SA(4), TBG(4), SVK(3), RKVS(2), SS(2), India(9) = 34 contributions + 51 others (1 each)
3.	Location/Distribution	142	DRS(14), SVK(6), TBG(6), KV(3), SKR(3), RBP(3), SE(3), JAG(2), JMM(2), KG(2), PC(2), SU(2), WS(2), SHM(2), NCAER(2), India(9) = 63 contributions + 79 others (1 each)
4.	Transport Network	35	DRS(6), TBG(5), India(9), = 20 contributions + 15 others (1 each)
5.	Typology	39	DRS(14), TBG(3), SVK(2), India(9) = 28 contributions + 11 others (1 each)
6.	Centrality/Hierarchy	41	DRS(9), SVK(3), SHO(2), SLR(2), India(9), = 25 contributions + 16 others (1 each)
7.	Trade Area	81	DRS(9), DAK(3), RBP(2), ASM(2), CAB(2), KG(2), SHM(2), SU(2), India(9) = 33 contributions + 48 others (1 each)
8.	Structure/Morphology	41	PC(3), SHM(3), SA(2), SJP(2), India(9) = 19 contributions + 22 others (1 each)
9.	Consumer/Trader Behaviour	43	DRS(6), DAK(4), SVK(3), CK(2), GDA(2), TBG(2), India(9) = 28 contributions + 15 others (1 each)
10.	Synchronization/Cycles	43	DRS(14), SVK(3), TBG(3), GDA(2), India(9) = 31 contributions + 12 others (1 each)
11.	Traditional Exchange	136	TBG(12), DRS(10), SVK(5), GDA(5), KV(3), SHM(3), SKR(3), WS(3), SE(3), CK(2), JAG(2), GK(2), TRC(2), RPP(2), India(9) = 66 contributions + 70 others (1 each)
12.	Urban/Regulated	93	DRS(6), SA(5), DAK(3), SHM(3), SLR(3), GPK(2), RKVS(2), RPP(2), WS(2), India(9) = 37 contributions + 56 others (1 each)
13.	Function	43	DRS(2), SA(2), India(9) = 13 contributions + 30 others (1 each)
14.	Goods/Commodities	66	RKC(2), RBP(2), SU(2), WS(2), India(9) = 17 contributions + 49 others (1 each)
15.	Planning	71	DRS(6), SLR(3), GPK(2), WS(2), NCAER(4), India(9) = 26 contributions + 45 others (1 each)
16.	Others	126	DRS(9), TBG(7), SVK(6), SA(3), SLR(3), VSC(2), SSB(2), RPB(2), SKR(2), JDC(2), SS(2), India(9) = 52 contributions + 74 others (1 each)

Abbreviations:

ASM (Alam, S.M.), CK (Chandran, K.), CAB (Chatterjee, A.B.), DRS (Dixit, R.S.), DAK (Dutta, A.K.), GDA (Gedam, D.A.), GPK (Gupta, P.K.), JAG (Jamkar, A.G.), JMM (Jana, M.M.), JDC (Jayashankar, D.C.), KG (Krishan, G.), KV (Krishnan, V), NCAER (National Council of Applied Economic Research), PC (Parvathi, C.), RKC (Ramakrishna, K.C.), RBP (Rao, B.P.), RKVS (Rao, K.V.S.), RPP (Rao, P.P.), SA (Sami, A.), SHM (Saxena, H.M.), SJP (Singh, J.P.), SLR (Singh, L.R.), SSB (Singh, S.B.), SU (Singh, U.), SHO (Srivastava, H.O.), SKR (Srivastava, K.R.), SVK (Srivastava, V.K.), SS (Subbaih, S.), SE (Swaminathan, E.), TBG (Tamaskar, B.G.), TRC (Tiwari, R.C.), VSC (Verma, S.C.), WS (Wanmali, S.).

RESEARCH ARTICLES : OTHERS ON INDIAN PERSPECTIVES

There are some very valuable research articles on marketing perspectives of the country presented by some other researchers among whom H.G. Bohle and B. Harriss are worth mention. As many as 27 such articles have been traced by the author. These articles appeared during the period 1930-1985 but most of the articles belong to the 1970s and 1980s. Table 8 gives some relevant details of these works.

TABLE 8 : RESEARCH ARTICLES – OTHERS ON INDIAN PERSPECTIVES

Scholar	*Year*	*Scholar*	*Year*
Armstrong, C.G.	1930, 1939	Hirt, H.F.	1975
Ash, W.C.	1933	Johnson, E.A.J.	1972
Astor, A.	1982	Joseph, S.E.	1972
Beatty, G.F.	1982	Master, M.A.	1953
Bohle, H.G.	1981a, 1981b, 1985	Miltendorf, H.J.	1982
Bradnock, R.W.	1974	Neale, W. *et al.*	1965
Fox, R.G.	1967, 1979	Warrior, S.K.	1972
Harriss, B.	1975, 1976, 1979 1980a, 1980b, 1981b, 1983a, 1983b, 1985		

Decadewise Break-up of Number of Articles:

1930s: (3)	**1970s: (9)**	**1980s: (12)**
1930	1972a	1980a
1933	1972b	1980b
1939	1972c	1981a
	1974	1981b
1950s: (1)	1975a	1981c
1953	1975b	1982a
	1976	1982b
1960s: (2)	1979a	1982c
1965	1979b	1983a
1967		1983b
		1985a
		1985b

RESEARCH CONTRIBUTIONS ON INDIAN PERSPECTIVES – CLASSIFIED

The author has made an attempt to classify the total research contributions which encompass various types of research pieces such as books, reports (dissertation and others), and articles (published papers, and unpublished papers, and abstracts) authored by the Indian scholars and others on marketing perspectives of the country. The total number of these researchers stands at 536 of which break - up is shown in Table 9(ii).

TABLE 9(i): MAJOR CONTRIBUTORS AND THEIR CONTRIBUTIONS

Contributor	*Coverage of Period*	*Number of Contributions*				
		Book	*Report*	*Paper*	*Unpublished Paper/Abstract*	*Total*
Dixit, R.S.	1977-1987	2	2	31	26	4+57
Harriss, B.	1975-1985	3		7	2	3+9
ICSSR	1972-1984	11				11
IGU	1973-1985	18				18
India	1979-1985					9
Sami, A.	1974-1980	1	1	7		2+7
Saxena, H.M.	1971-1985	2	2	8	2	4+10
Singh, J	1975-1980			5		5
Singh, L.R.	1980-1986			6	3	9
Srivastava, V.K.	1971-1987	3	1	13	3	4+16
Tamaskar, B.G.	1956-1985		1	16	1	1+17

TABLE 9(ii): TOTAL CONTRIBUTIONS

Books (See Tables 3 and 4)	:	41 +29	= 70	Total = 536
Reports (See Tables 5 and 6)	:	29 +12	= 41	
Papers (See Tables 7(ii) and 8	:	302 +24	= 326	
Unpublished/Abstracts	:	96 + 3	= 99	
Indian Scholars' Research Articles	:	302 +96	= 398	(See Table 7(i)
Others : Research Articles	:	24 + 3	= 27	(See Table 8)
Indian Scholars' Reports	:	29 +12	= 41	(See Tables 5 & 6)
Indian Scholars' Books	:	41	= 41	(See Table 3)
Others : Books	:	29	= 29	(See Table 4)
Total Number of Books and Reports		(111) +		
Papers and Abstracts		(425)		
			536	

These contributions have been listed in alphabetical (author_wise) order in the bibliography.

BIBLIOGRAPHY

At the end of the inventory, the author has supplied with an exhaustive bibliography listing all the researches done by the Indian scholars and others on various perspectives of the marketing panorama of the country. The bibliography, thus, consists of about 550 such entries arranged in alphabetical order (author-wise).

2

REVIEWS AND BIBLIOGRAPHIES ON LITERATURE – THE WORLD CONTEXT

(Alphabetical Order)

Applebaum, W. (1954) Marketing geography, in James, P.E. and Jones, C.F. (eds.), *American Geography: Inventory and Prospects*, Syracuse University, 245-51.

Applebaum, W. and Selapken, B.L. (1955) *Atlas of Business Centres*, Cincinati, Hamilton County.

Bromley, R.J. (1971) Markets in the developing countries - A review, *Geography*, 50, 124-132.

Bromley, R.J. (1974a) *Market Place Studies: A World Bibliography Upto 1972*, London School of Oriental and African Studies.

Bromley, R.J. (1974b) *Periodic Market, Daily Market, and Fairs: A Bibliography*, Monash Publication in Geography, No. 10, Melbourne, Monash University.

Bromley, R.J. (1979) *Periodic Market, Daily Market, and Fairs: A Bibliography, Supplement to 1974*, Centre for Development Studies, Swansea, University College.

Murphy, R.E. (1961) Marketing geography comes of age, *Store Location and Development Studies*, A Volume of reprints from Economic Geography, 37.

Smith, R.H.T. (1979) Periodic market places and periodic marketing - A review and prospects : I, *Progress in Human Geography*, 3(4), 471-505.

Smith, R.H.T. (1980) Periodic market places and periodic marketing - A review and prospects : II, *Progress in Human Geography*, 4(1), 1-31.

SECTION B

INVENTORY – THE INDIAN CONTEXT

3

REVIEWS AND BIBLIOGRAPHIES ON LITERATURE

(Chronological Order)

1972 : Shafi, M. Geography of transport and marketing: A trend report, in *A Survey of Research in Geography*, Bombay, Popular Prakashan, 84-85 and 361-62.

1977 : Saxena, H.M. Marketing geography: A review, *The Deccan Geographer*, 15(1), 250-56.

1979 : Singh, J. Geography of transport and marketing, in *Survey of Research in Geography (1969-72)*, New Delhi, Allied Publishers, 53-60.

1980 : Dixit, R.S. and Verma, D.N. Marketing geography: A bibliographic note, *Uttar Bharat Bhugol Patrika*, 16(1), 70-78.

1980 : Sami, A. The geography of retailing: A coceptual review, in R.B. Mandal and V.N.P. Sinha (eds.) *Recent Trends and Concepts in Geography*, Vol. II, New Delhi, Concept Publishing Company, 151-69.

1980 : Saxena, H.M. Marketing geography - Concepts and trends, in R.B. Mandal and V.N.P. Sinha (eds.) *Recent Trends and Concepts in Geography*, Vol. II, New Delhi, Concept Publishing Company, 141-49.

1980 : Singh, L.R. *Recent Trends in Indian Geography*, Presidential Address, Silver Jubilee Session, Indian Council of Geographers, 1-42.

1982 : Compiled, *Who's Who of Geographers in India*, New Delhi, Concept Publishing Company, 132.

1983 : Arunachalam, B. The Geography of rural markets in India: An inventory and prospect, *Proceedings of Symposium on Impact of Weekly Markets on Rural Societies*, Geography Department, Madurai University, October 7-10.

1983 : Sinha, B.N. *Progress of Geographical Research in India : Approved Theses in Indian Universities*, Transactions - Indian Council of Geographers, 11, 1-38.

1984a : Dixit, R.S. *Market Centres and their Spatial Development in the Umland of Kanpur*, Allahabad, Kitab Mahal, 1-25.

1984b : Dixit, R.S. *Spatial Organisation of Market Centres in Hamirpur District, U.P. India*, Research Project Report of the Indian Council of Social Science Research, New Delhi.

1984 : Jayashankar, D.C. Marketing geography, in *A Survey of Research in Geography (1972-75)*, New Delhi, Concept Publishing Company, 41-50.

1984 : Sinha, B.N. *Progress of Geographical Research in India: Topics Registered for Ph.D. in Geography in Indian Universities*, Transaction - Indian Council of Geographers, 13, 1-40.

1984 : Srivastava, V.K. Progress of marketing geography in India, *The Indian Journal of Marketing Geography*, 2(1-2), 1-13.

1984 : Tiwari, R.C. and Tripathi, S. Vipanan bhugol, *Bhu Sangam*, 2(1), 45-56.

1985 : Gormsen, E. *Market Place Research*, Mainz, Geographisches Insitut der Johannes - Gutenberg Universitat, 71-124.

1985 : Ishihara, H. *Rural Markets in South India*, School of Letters, University of Nagoya, 1-25.

1985 : Srivastava, V.K. Geography of commercial activities: A trend report, *Proceedings of International Conference on Commercial Activities and Rural Development*, Geography Department, Gorakhpur University, December 23-25.

1986 : Dixit, R.S. Geography of commercial activities, *The Indian National Geographer*, 1(1-2), 98-108.

1986a : Metton, A. *Geography of Commercial Activities*, Newsletter No. 1, International Geographical Union, Study Group, January, 1-20.

1986b : Metton, A. *Geography of Commercial Activities*, Newsletter No. 2, International Geographical Union, Study Group, June, 1-8.

1986 : Sinha, B.N. *Trends in Geographical Research in India*, Bhubaneswar, Indian Council of Geographers, 1-158.

1987 : Metton, A. *Geography of Commercial Activities*, Newsletter No. 3, International Geographical Union, Study Group, January, 1-33.

Undated : ICSSR *Marketing in Terms of Geography: A Bibliography*, New Delhi, Indian Council of Social Science Research.

Note :Recently completed works are as follows:

1988 : Dixit, R.S. *Spatial Organization of Market Centres*, Jaipur, Pointer, 9-25.

1988 : Ishihara, H. *Markets and Marketing in South India*, Nagoya, School of Letters, University of Nagoya.

1989 : Ishihara, H. *Markets and Marketing in West Bengal and East Nepal*, Nagoya, School of Letters, University of Nagoya.

4

RESEARCH BOOKS AND MONOGRAPHS–I

(Chronological Order)

1930 : Pant, D. *The Commercial Policy of Moghuls*, Bombay.

1937 : Hussain, S.A. *Agricutural Marketing in Northern India*, London, George Allan and Unwin.

1951 : Kulkarni, K.R. *Agricultural Marketing in India*, 2 volumes, Bombay, Co-operative Book Depot.

1953 : Mitra, A. *Fairs and Festivals in Western Bengal*, Alipore, Government Press.

1956 : Barunu, H. and Baneja, J.D. *The Fairs and Festivals of Assam*, Gauhati, D.N. Dutta, Baranu.

1965a : NCAER *Market Towns and Spatial Development in India*, New Delhi, National Council of Applied Economic Research.

1965b : NCAER *Techno-Economic Survey of Uttar Pradesh*, New Delhi, National Council of Applied Economic Research.

1968 : Sinha, D.P. *Culture Change in an Inter-tribal Market*, Bombay, Asia Publishing House.

1971 : Rao, B.P. *Vishakhapatnam - A Study in Geography of Port-Town*, The National Geographical Society of India.

1972 : ICSSR *A Survey of Research in Geography*, Bombay, Popular Prakashan.

1972 : NCAER *Market Towns and Spatial Development*, New Delhi, National Council of Applied Economic Research.

1974 : Sinha, B.N. *Trade and Industrial Market of Bihar*, Patna, Arvind Publications.

1975 : Chaudhary, S. *Trade and Commercial Organisation in Bengal (1650-1720) with Special Reference to English East India Company*, Calcutta.

1975-82 : ICSSR *Journal of Abstracts and Reviews - Geography*, 8 volumes, 1975 to 1982, New Delhi, Concept Publishing Company.

1975 : Saxena, H.M. *Geography of Transport and Market Centres - A Case Study of Hadaoti Plateau*, New Delhi, S. Chand & Co.

1978 : Pal, M.K. *Crafts and Craftsmen in Traditional India*, New Delhi, Kanak Publications.

1979 : Dixit, R.S. *Glimpses of the Umland of an Indian Metropolis - The Case of Kanpur*, Lucknow, Mrs. Asha Dixit/Vikas-Sheel Bhugol Parishad.

1979 : ICSSR *A Survey of Research in Geography (1969-72)*, New Delhi, Allied Publishers, for the Indian Council of Social Science Research.

1979 : Leon, S. *The North Indian Peasant Goes to Market*, Delhi, Motilal Banarsidas.

1980 : Sami, A. *Intra-Urban Market Geography*, New Delhi, Concept Publishing Company.

1980 : Wanmali, S. *Periodic Markets and Rural Development in India – A Case Study of Singhbhum District*, Bihar, New Delhi, Concept Publishing Company.

1982 : CONCEPT *Who's Who of Geographers in India*, New Delhi, Concept Publishing Company.

1982 : Ramachandran, H. *Behaviour in Space - Rural Marketing in Under Developed Economy* New Delhi, Concept Publishing Company.

1983 : Sinha, B.N. *Progress of Geographical Research in India*, Transaction - Indian Council of Geographers, 11, December.

1983 : Srivastava, V.K. *Market Studies*, The Association of Marketing Geographers, India.

1984 : Dixit, R.S. *Market Centres and their Spatial Development in the Umland of Kanpur*, Allahabad, Kitab Mahal.

1984 : ICSSR *A Survey of Research in Geography (1972-75)*, New Delhi, Concept Publishing Company.

1984 : Saxena, H.M. *Geography of Marketing*, New Delhi, Sterling Publishers.

1984 : Sinha, B.N. *Progress of Geographical Research in India*, Transaction - Indian Council of Geographers, 13, December.

1984 : Srivastava, V.K. *The Indian Journal of Marketing Geography*, The Association of Marketing Geographers, India.

1985 : ICRISAT *Agricultural Markets in the Semi-Arid Tropics*, Patancheru, International Crop Research Institute for the Semi-Arid Tropics.

1986 : Sinha, B.N. *Trends in Geographical Research in India*, Bhubaneswar, Indian Council of Geographers.

1987 : Srivastava, V.K. *Geography of Marketing and Rural Develop-*

ment, New Delhi, Inter-India Publications.

Undated : *India - Survey Report on Rural Market Development Programme*, New Delhi.

Note: Recently completed works are as follows.

1988 : Dixit, R.S. *Spatial Organization of Market Centres*, Jaipur, Pointer.

1988 : Srivastava, V.K.(ed.) *Commercial Activities and Rural Development in South Asia*, New Delhi, Concept Publishing Company.

5

RESEARCH BOOKS AND MONOGRAPHS II

OTHERS ON INDIAN PERSPECTIVES

(Chronological Order)

1929 : Bentley, O.A. *Fairs and Festivals in Bengal.*

1961 : Ishihara, H. Markets in West Bengal: An Analysis of District Census Handbook, *The Journal of the Faculty of Literature*, Nagoya University, Vol. 80.

1972-85 : IGU *Newsletters of the International Geographical Union Working Group on Market Place Exchange Systems*, Vancouver, University of British Columbia, 15 Volumes.

1978 : Ishihara, H. Markets in Howrah District, West Bengal, in *Professor Fujioka's Commemoration Historico-Geographical Studies and Urban Studies*, Tokyo, Taimeido Publication.

1979 : Ishihara, H. Markets in Hooghly District, West Bengal, *The Journal of the Faculty of Literature*, Nagoya University, The Thirtieth Anniversary Volume.

1981 : Harriss, B. *Traditional Trade and Rural Development*, New Delhi, Vikas Publishing House.

1983a : Ishihara, H. Traditional Markets and Areal Demand Density in India, *The Journal of the Faculty of Literature*, Nagoya University, Volume 83.

1983b : Ishihara, H. Distribution of Markets in India and Bangladesh, *The Journal of the Faculty of Literature*, Nagoya University, Volume 86.

1984a : Harriss, B. *Exchange Relations and Poverty in Dryland Agriculture*, New Delhi, Concept Publishing Company.

1984b : Harriss, B. *State and Market - State Intervention in Agricultural Exchange in a Dry Region of Tamil Nadu*, New Delhi, Concept Publishing Company.

1985a : Ishihara, H. *General Survey of Traditional Markets in Tamil Nadu, South India, Professor J. Hosai Commemoration chiiki o mequru.*

1985b : Ishihara, H. *Rural Markets in South India*, Nagoya University, School of Letters, August

1986-87 : IGU *Newsletters of the International Geographical Union Study Group: Geography of Commercial Activities*, 3 Volumes.

Note: Recently completed works are as follows:

1988 : Ishihara, H. *Markets and Marketing in South India*, Nagoya, School of Letters, University of Nagoya.

1989 : Ishihara, H. *Markets and Marketing in West Bengal and East Nepal*, Nagoya, School of Letters, University of Nagoya.

6

RESEARCH PROJECT REPORTS - I

DISSERTATIONS

(Chronological Order)

1958 : Singh, S.M. *Rural Markets and Urban Settlements in the District of Faizabad*, M.A. Dissertation, Geography Department, Banaras Hindu University.

1959 : Rao, R. *Regulated Markets in India with Special Reference to Andhra Pradesh*, D. Phil. Dissertation, Allahabad University.

1963 : Singh, K.N. *Rural Markets and Rurban Centres in Eastern U.P. – A Geographical Analysis*, Ph. D. Dissertation, Geography Department, Banaras Hindu University.

1964 : Barnum, H. *A Model of the Markets for Foodgrains in India*, Ph.D. Dissertation, Berkley, University of California.

1964 : Sinha, D.P. *The Role of Banari-Intertribal Market among the Hill People of Chhota Nagpur - A Study in Cultural Change*, Ph.D. Dissertation, South Illinois University.

1966 : Vishwanath, M.S. *A Geographical Analysis of Rural Markets and Rurban Centres in Mysore*, Ph.D. Dissertation, Geography Department, Banaras Hindu University.

1968 : Sinha, M.K. *Spatial Distribution of Retail Trade - A Case Study of Patna*, M.C.P. Dissertation, Kharagpur, Indian Institute of Technology.

1971 : Saxena, H.M. *Geography of Transport and Market Centres - A Case Study of Hadaoti Plateau*, Ph. D. Dissertation, Geography Department, Udaipur University.

1973 : Kumavat, B.L. *Market Towns of the Central Aravali*, Ph. D. Dissertation, Geography Department, Udaipur University.

1975 : Sami, A. *Functional Spatial Analysis of Markets of Patna*, Ph. D. Dissertation, Geography Department, Patna University.

1976 : Nolakha, R.L. *Marketing of Handicraft in Rajasthan*, Ph. D. Dissertation, Rajasthan University.

1976 : Swaminathan, E. *Market Centres and Consumer Preference with Coimbatore Metropolitan Area*, Ph. D. Dissertation, Geography Department, Madras University.

1977 : Geetha, T. *A Spatial Analysis of Periodic Markets in Krishnagiri Taluk*, M. Phil. Dissertation, Faculty of Science, Madras University.

1978 : Chandran, K. *An Analysis of Marketing Functions in Weekly Markets - The Case Study of Shivaganga*, M.Phil. Dissertation, Geography Department, Madurai University.

1978-79 : Gedam, D.A. *The Marketing System and Network in the Wardha Valley*, Ph. D. Dissertation, Geography Department, Nagpur University.

1978 : Parvathi, C. *Market Centres and Spatial Development - A Case Study of Coimbatore-Nilgiri Region*, Ph. D. Dissertation, Geography Department, Mysore University.

1978 : Wanmali, S. *Periodic Markets in South Bihar*, Ph. D. Dissertation, University of Cambridge.

1979 : Dixit, R.S. *Market Centres and their Spatial Development in the Umland of Kanpur*, D. Phil. Dissertation, Geography Department, Allahabad University.

1979 : Maidamwar, G.T. *Livestock Marketing Network and System in Yavatmal District*, Ph. D. Dissertation, Geography Department, Nagpur University.

1979 : Rathore, N.S. *Regulated Markets in Rajasthan - A Critical Study in Organisation and Working*, Ph. D. Dissertation, Udaipur University.

1979 : Vishwanath, V.V. *Functional Analysis of Wholesale Marketing of Grains and Vegetables in Madras City*, Ph. D. Dissertation, Geography Department, Madras University.

1979 : Dixit, R.S. *Market Centres and their Spatial Development in the Umland of Kanpur*, D. Phil. Dissertation, Geography Department, Allahabad University.

1980 : Mohanty, S.K. *Hierarchy of Market Centres in Lower Mahanadi-Brahmani Basin*, Ph. D. Dissertation, Geography Department, Utkal University.

1980 : Srivastava, H.O. *Geography of Market Centres in Saryupar Plain, U.P.*, Ph. D. Dissertation, Geography Department, Gorakhpur University.

1982 : Ram, U. *Periodic Markets and Rural Development in the Lower Ganga-Ghagra Doab*, Ph. D. Dissertation, Geography Department, Gorakhpur University.

1983 : Nath, V. *Marketing and Social Structure in North Avadh Plain*, Ph. D. Dissertation, Geography Department, Gorakhpur University.

1983 : Sharma, P.K. *Market Centres in Central Assam - A Geographical Analysis*, Ph. D. Dissertation, Geography Department, Utkal University.

1983 : Srivastava, K.R. *Periodic Markets and Central Places in Baghelkhand Region*, Ph. D. Dissertation, Geography Department, Jabalpur University.

1984 : Hugar, S.I. *Spatial Analysis of Market Systems in Dharwad District*, Ph. D. Dissertation, Geography Department, Karnatak University.

1987 : Verma, R.D. *Analysis of Periodic Market Centres in Pratapgarh District*, Ph. D. Dissertation, Geography Department, Kanpur University.

Note: Also see Doctoral and Post-Doctoral Research Projects (in progress/recently completed) in Chapter 13.

7

RESEARCH PROJECT REPORTS - II

OTHER THAN DISSERTATIONS

(Chronological Order)

1961 : Prakash Rao, V.S.L. *Bongiri - A Case Study in Market Town*, Census of India Monograph No. 12, New Delhi, Registrar General, Ministry of Health.

1967 : Khan, W. *Market Settlements in Hyderabad Metropolitan Region*, Technical Bulletin No. 5, Hyderabad, Metropolitan Research Project.

1970 : Karwe, I. and Acharya, H. *The Role of Weekly Markets - in the Tribal, Rural, and Urban Setting*, Research Project Report, New Delhi, Indian Council of Social Science Research.

1971 : Joshi, V.K. *Regular Markets in Gujarat*, Sardar Patel University.

1978-79 : Tamaskar, B.G. *The Periodic Marketing System and Network on the Arvi Upland*, Research Project Report, New Delhi, University Grants Commission.

1980 : Patil, S.P. and Pawat, J.R. *A Study of Marketing of Fruits in Mahatona Phule Market Bombay*, Department of Agricultural Economics, Mahatona Phule Krishi.

1980 : Raju, V.T. and Open, M. von *Market Channels for Selected Crops in Semi-Arid Tropical India*, Economic Programme Progress Report, No. 16, Patancheru, International Crop Research Institute for the Semi-Arid Tropics.

1980 : Saxena, H.M. *Geographical Study of Market Towns in Rajasthan*, Research Project Report, New Delhi, Indian Council of Social Science Research.

1982 : Raju, V.T. and Open, M. von *Marketing Efficiency for Selected Crops in the Semi-Arid Tropical India*, Economic Programme Progress Report, No. 32, Patancheru, International Crop Research Institute for the Semi-Arid Tropics.

1982 : Srivastava, V.K. *Geography of Market Centres in the Tarai*

Region of U.P., Research Project Report, New Delhi, Indian Council of Social Science Research.

1983 : Wanmali, S. *Service Provision and Rural Development in India – A Case Study of Miryal Guda Taluk*, Research Project Report, No. 37, Washington D.C., International Food Research Institute.

1984 : Dixit, R.S. *Spatial Organisation of Market Centres in Hamirpur District, U.P. (India)*, Research Project Report, New Delhi, Indian Council of Social Science Research.

Note :Recently completed works are as follows:

1988 : Dixit, R.S. *Marketing Geography: The Indian Scenario - Inventory and Prospects*, Research Project Report, New Delhi, Indian Council of Social Science Research.

1989 : Dixit, R.S. *Periodic Marketing in an Urban Environment Mahoba: A Case Study in Geography of Commercial Activities*, Research Project Report, New Delhi, University Grants Commission.

8 (I)

RESEARCH ARTICLES - I

THEMATIC TYPOLOGY - A

(Chronological Order)

Nature and Perspectives : 1. Role, 2. Origin/Evolution, 3. Location/Distribution, 4. Transport Network, 5. Typology, 6. Centrality/Hierarchy, 7. Trade Area, 8. Structure/Morphology, 9. Consumer/Trader Behaviour, 10. Synchronization/Rings, 11. Traditional Exchange/Periodic Marketing, 12. Urban or daily/Agricultural or Regulated Marketing, 13. Function, 14. Goods/Commodities, 15. Planning Perspective, 16. Others.

Year	Scholar	Study Area	Nature and Perspectives															
			1	2	3	4	5	6	7	8	9	10	11	12	13	14	15	16
1931	Ramakrishna, K.C.	Malabar			*				*							*		
1932	Krishnan, V.	Madurai-Ramnad			*								*					
1933	Krishnan, V.	Trichy			*								*					
1933	Paul, M.S.	Udayapalayam			*								*			*		
1937	Pandyan, S.R.	Nagapatnam																
1938	Punja, H.G.	Mangalore							*							*		
1938	Ramamurthy, K.	Madras							*							*		
1939	Ramakrishna, K.C.	Madras														*		
1940	Krishnan, V.	Tinnevelly			*								*			*		
1940	Ponnaiah, J.S.	Tinnevelly			*				*				*	*		*		
1940	Thyagarajan, V.	Tuticorin			*											*		
1941	Agarwala, V.S.								*						*	*		
1941	Deshpande, C.D.	Bombay-Karnatak			*				*				*					
1941	Mathur, V.S.	Wn.United Provinces											*	*				
1942	Swami, P.												*					
1949	Bose, N.K.				*											*		
1951	Sinha, S.	Bamnia-Manbhum											*					
1953	Pattanaik, N.	Barpalli											*					
1955	Mukherjee, A.B.	Central Bhirbhum							*							*		
1955	Ramanandham, V.V.	Andhra Pradesh			*				*							*		
1955	Tamaskar, B.G.	Patharia Kalan											*					
1957	Deb, A.K.	West bengal		*	*				*							*		
1957	Mukherjee, A.B.	Modinagar			*								*					
1959	Singh, U.	Allahabad		*	*				*				*			*		
1960	Singh, U.	Allahabad			*				*						*	*		

Year	Scholar	Study Area	Nature and Perspectives															
			1	2	3	4	5	6	7	8	9	10	11	12	13	14	15	16
1961	Reddy, S.N.	Hyderabad	*	*	*											*		
1961	Singh, K.N.	Barhaj	*	*						*				*	*	*		
1961	Sinha, S.N.	Bamni	*	*									*					
1962	Janki, V.K.	Baroda		*					*									
1963	Kulkarni, G.S.	Yamakanmardi			*				*									
1963	Alam, S.M.	Hyderabad-Sec'bad							*	*				*	*			
1963	Jayaswal, S.N.P.	Bindki	*	*	*				*									
1963	Kayastha, S.L.	Kandla	*	*	*													
1963	Krishan, G.	Chandigarh			*				*							*		
1963	Patel, A.M.	Rajshahi	*	*	*								*					
1963	Sinha, D.P.	Pharia	*	*	*													
1963	Veeranna, S.													*			*	
1965	Chatterjee, A.B.	Howrah			*				*					*				
1965	Singh, H. *et al*.	Kurali	*	*	*				*						*	*		
1965	Singh, S.M.	Faizabad		*														
1965	Tamaskar, B.G.	Garhakota											*					
1966a	Dutta, A.K.	Calcutta							*		*			*				
1966b	Dutta, A.K.	Howrah							*		*			*				
1966	Rao, R.B.	Vishakhapatnam			*				*							*		
1966a	Tamaskar, B.G.	Sagar-Damoh			*	*	*						*				*	
1966b	Tamaskar, B.G.	Sagar-Damoh			*	*	*						*					
1967	Gupta, S.K.	Baraut		*	*				*							*		
1967	Rao, B.P	Cochin			*				*						*	*		
1967	Singh, A.																	*
1968	Agarwala, P.C.	Bastar	*	*	*	*			*				*					

Year	Scholar	Study Area	Nature and Perspectives															
			1	2	3	4	5	6	7	8	9	10	11	12	13	14	15	16
1968	Das, M.	Calcutta		*	*				*							*		
1968	Mukherjee, S.P.	Darjeeling			*		*	*							*			
1968	Thakur, B.	Patna			*				*						*	*		
1968	Verma, L.N.	Jhalrapatan			*					*			*					
1969	Chatterjee, A.B.	Calcutta				*			*		*					*		
1969	Ramakrishnan, N.	Tamil Nadu			*				*				*		*	*		
1969	Rao, B.P.			*	*	*										*		
1970	Mukherjee, M.	Bihar		*	*				*						*	*		
1971	NCAER		*	*	*	*	*	*	*	*	*	*	*	*	*	*		*
1971	Raza, M.	Bihar			*				*	*			*		*			
1971	Srivastava, V.K.	Upper Son Basin			*				*						*			
1971	Suresh, R.	Kanpur			*								*	*				
1971	Verghese, I.	Mysore			*				*				*	*				
1972	Aherwadkar, L.J.	Marathawada	*	*										*				
1972	Andrade, C.P.	Khanna	*	*										*				
1972	Bawa, R.L.	North Bihar															*	
1972	Bedekar, S.L.		*	*		*											*	
1972	Bhat, L.S.	India															*	
1972	Bhawmik, K.L.	Sunderban/Cal	*		*	*											*	
1972	Bose, A.N.	West Bengal															*	
1972	Bumb, B.L.	Udaipur												*				
1972a	Dutta, A.K.	Calcutta							*		*			*	*	*		
1972b	Dutta, A.K.	Calcutta									*							
1972a	Garg, P.K.	India												*			*	
1972b	Garg, P.K.	India												*	*		*	

Year	Scholar	Study Area	Nature and Perspectives															
			1	2	3	4	5	6	7	8	9	10	11	12	13	14	15	16
1972	Ghosal, K.			*	*		*	*	*									*
1972	Gupta, N.L.	Rajasthan			*				*						*	*		
1972	Gupta, V.K.	India															*	
1972	Hashin, S.r.	Gujrat						*							*			
1972	Kahlon, S.S.	Punjab	*	*	*												*	
1972	Khan, W.	Chevella, A.P.											*					
1972	Kulkarni, G.S.	Western India				*		*										*
1972	Lahiri, T.B.	India	*		*													*
1972	Mahalanobis, J.N.																*	
1972	Maikap, A.K.	West Bengal	*		*											*	*	
1972	Mathai, P.M.	India	*		*								*	*			*	
1972	Mathur, G.C.																*	
1972	Mohanty, P.	Parlekhabedi			*									*				
1972	Muthiah, C.	Madras												*			*	
1972a	NCAER				*												*	
1972b	NCAER		*														*	
1972c	NCAER		*														*	
1972d	NCAER																*	
1972	Rao, P.P.																*	
1972	Reddy, N.V.	Rayalaseema															*	
1972	Sarkar, A.K.		*														*	
1972	Saxena, H.M.	Hadaoti Plateau			*			*					*					
1972	Selvam, L.G.																*	
1972	Shafi, M.																	*
1972	Shah, S.M.																*	

Year	Scholar	Study Area	1	2	3	4	5	6	7	8	9	10	11	12	13	14	15	16
			Nature and Perspectives															
1972	Singh, A.J.	Punjab			*									*				
1972	Singh, S.K.	Lar (Deoria)	*	*													*	
1972	Suri, K.B.	India		*														
1972	Talwar, B.R.	Punjab															*	
1972	Venugopal, V.	Warangal, A.P.			*					*								
1972	Vepa, R.K.		*	*													*	
1972	Vishwanath, M.S.			*										*			*	
1973	Bhattacharya, B.N.	North Bengal	*	*	*													
1973	Chandra, R.	M.P.											*					*
1973	Krishan, G., *et al.*	Chandigarh								*				*				
1973	Mahalay, K.L.	Deccan Caves	*	*														*
1974	Duggal, S.L., *et al.*	Haryána					*							*				
1974	Gedam, D.A.	Salbardi						*	*	*			*					
1974	Lal, R.S.	Revalganj	*														*	*
1974	Mahato, S.N.	Ranchi	*		*			*							*	*		
1974	Sami, A.	Patna								*				*				
1974	Saxena, H.M.	Kota								*								
1974	Sinha, V.N.P.	Bihar			*			*	*									
1974	Srivastava, K.R.			*	*				*	*			*	*				*
1974	Thakur, B.										*			*				
1974	Chakravarty, T.	Calcutta		*											*	*		
1974	Das, P.K.	Nand Kumar							*									*
1975	Das, T.K.	Memari, W.Bengal	*														*	*
1975	Jain, N.G.	Nagpur West			*				*				*	*			*	*
1975a	Parvathi, C.	Pollachi			*					*								

Year	Scholar	Study Area	Nature and Perspectives															
			1	2	3	4	5	6	7	8	9	10	11	12	13	14	15	16
1975b	Parvathi, C.	Pollachi								*								
1975	Patil, B.	Bijapur		*										*			*	*
1975	Prasad, I.	Sainthia, Birbhum			*	*			*									
1975a	Sami, A.	Patna		*						*				*				
1975b	Sami, A.	Patna			*										*			*
1975	Singh, J.	Bihar			*									*		*		
1975	Singh, J.P.	Shillong			*			*		*								
1976	Dayal, P. and Thakur, B.	Patna		*					*	*				*	*			
1976	Jayashankar, D.C.	Madras		*					*									*
1976	Kala, S.C.	U.P.												*				
1976	Parvathi, C.	Pollachi			*				*	*			*					
1976	Sami,A.	Patna		*										*				*
1976	Sharma, B.D.	Tribal Areas			*				*						*	*		*
1976	Singh, R.B. and Singh, K.K.	Maya Bazar			*										*	*		*
1976	Sita, K.	South Konkan			*								*					
1976	Srivastava, K.R.	Meerut			*								*					
1976a	Srivastava, V.K.	Baghelkhand Plateau			*													*
1976b	Srivastava, V.K.	Naugarh						*										*
1976	Wanmali, S.	Singhbhum, S.Bihar			*											*		
1977	Banrod, R.G.												*					*
1977	Baruah, S.L.	Assam		*	*			*		*								
1977	Dixit, R.S.	Kanpur			*				*						*			
1977	Hall, K.	South India						*										*
1977	Kumar, A. and Sharma, N.	Sundega													*			*
1977	Moharana, B.B.	Orissa			*								*					*

Year	Scholar	Study Area	1	2	3	4	5	6	7	8	9	10	11	12	13	14	15	16
			Nature and Perspectives															
1977	Saxena, H.M.																	*
1977	Shasmal, K.C.	Sundarbans, W.Bengal			*								*					*
1977	Singh, R.L. and Singh, R.P.B.									*			*					*
1977	Srivastava, V.K.	Bahraich	*	*	*							*						
1977	Tamaskar, B.G.	Maharashtra		*							*		*					*
1978	Agarwal, B.C.					*												*
1978	Aneja, R.K.																	*
1978	Bhagbati, A.K.	Kaithal Kunchi		*														*
1978	Geetha, T.	Krishnagiri							*				*					
1978	Jana, M.M.	Silabati Basin		*	*		*	*	*									
1978	Prasad, A.	Andhra Pradesh			*									*				
1978	Sami, A.	Patna		*										*	*			
1978	Singh, J.	Gorakhpur						*			*		*					
1978	Srivastava, V.K.	Bansi, U.P.					*				*	*	*					
1978	Srivastava, V.K. and Rai, J.P.	Ghosi, U.P.						*										*
1978	Tamaskar, B.G.	Chhatisgarh Plain		*	*				*			*	*					
1978	Uppal, J.S.		*											*				
1979	De, J.				*											*		*
1979	INDIA		*	*	*	*	*	*	*	*	*	*	*	*	*	*	*	*
1979	Jayashankar, D.C.	Karnataka															*	
1979	Maidamwar, G.T.	Yavatmal								*			*					*
1979	Malshe, P.T.		*							*			*					*
1979	Saxena, H.M.	Sriganganagar								*								*
1979	Setharam, K. and Chakraborty, S.C.	India				*		*	*							*		*

Year	Scholar	Study Area	Nature and Perspectives															
			1	2	3	4	5	6	7	8	9	10	11	12	13	14	15	16
1979	Singh, J.																	*
1979	Singhal, R.C.												*				*	*
1979	Srivastava, R.C. and Gupta, J.P.	Kanpur					*				*	*	*	*				
1979	Srivastava, V.K. and Srivastava, H.O.	Saryupar Plain			*		*						*					
1979a	Tamaskar, B.G.					*							*					*
1979b	Tamaskar, B.G.	Chhattisgarh Plain		*	*			*				*	*					
1979c	Tamaskar, B.G.	Chhattisgarh Plain				*							*					*
1979	Uppal, J.S.	Vridhachalam, South Arcot											*				*	*
1979	Vishwanath, V.V.			*	*								*			*		*
1979	Wanmali, S.		*	*									*	*			*	
1980	Chandran, K.	Shivganga, Tamil Nadu									*	*	*					
1980a	Dixit, R.S.		*															*
1980b	Dixit, R.S.	Kanpur				*												
1980c	Dixit, R.S.	Bundelkhand										*						
1980d	Dixit, R.S.																	*
1980e	Dixit, R.S.		*	*	*		*	*	*	*	*	*	*	*	*	*	*	*
1980f	Dixit, R.S.	Kanpur						*										
1980g	Dixit, R.S.		*														*	
1980h	Dixit, R.S.	Kanpur										*						
1980	Gedam, D.A.	Wardha Valley						*										
1980	INDIA		*	*	*	*	*	*	*	*	*	*	*	*	*	*	*	*
1980	Kulkarni, K.M.	Nasik		*	*					*				*				
1980a	Kumar, S.		*															*
1980b	Kumar, S.										*							

Year	Scholar	Study Area	1	2	3	4	5	6	7	8	9	10	11	12	13	14	15	16
			Nature and Perspectives															
1980	Mehtra, I.	North Indian village											*					
1980	Mohanty, S.K. and Singh, D.K.	Mahanadi-Brahmani Basin																*
1980	Raza, M.					*								*		*		
1980a	Sami, A.	Patna							*					*				
1980b	Sami, A.																	*
1980a	SAxena, H.M.	Sriganganagar									*	*		*				
1980b	Saxena, H.M.																	*
1980	Shafi, M.	Islamic World			*											*		
1980	Sharma, S.K. and Archana		*														*	
1980	Singh, J.P.	Shillong	*							*								*
1980a	Singh, L.R.																	*
1980b	Singh, L.R.																	*
1980	Singh, L.R. and Dixit, R.S.	Kanpur						*										
1980	Srivastava, H.O. and Srivastava, V.K.	Ganga-Ghaghra Doab						*										*
1980	Srivastava, V.K. and Nayak, H.P.			*	*	*												
1980	Vasudeo, Rao D.		*		*								*				*	
1980	Verma, R.V.	Shafipur, Unnao	*		*				*			*	*					
1980	Verma, S.C.		*	*	*				*			*					*	*
1980	Wanmali, S.		*										*	*			*	
1981	Aiyasami, U., *et al.*																	*
1981a	Dixit, R.S.	Kanpur					*											
1981b	Dixit, R.S.	Kanpur	*					*										
1981c	Dixit, R.S.	Kanpur				*												
1981d	Dixit, R.S.	Kanpur				*											*	

Year	Scholar	Study Area	Nature and Perspectives															
			1	2	3	4	5	6	7	8	9	10	11	12	13	14	15	16
1981e	Dixit, R.S.	Kanpur				*												
1981f	Dixit, R.S.	Bundelkhand										*						
1981g	Dixit, R.S.	Kanpur					*											
1981h	Dixit, R.S.	Kanpur			*													
1981i	Dixit, R.S.	Kanpur										*						
1981j	Dixit, R.S.	Kanpur		*								*	*					
1981	Gedam, D.A.	Wardha Valley	*	*									*					
1981	Katiyar, R.C.	Hamirpur						*										*
1981	Mani, K.C.													*				*
1981	Narayam, B.S.	Kerala	*	*										*				
1981	Nath, V. and Jain, A.K.	Avadh Plain											*					
1981	Sharma, R.C. and Kumar, A.	Kannauj			*													*
1981	Srivastava, V.K.	Uttar Pradesh			*									*				
1981	Tamaskar, B.G.	Arvi Upland			*													*
1982	Bose, P.K.	Gujrat			*	*										*		*
1982a	Dixit, R.S.	Kanpur							*									
1982b	Dixit, R.S.	Bundelkhand										*						
1982c	Dixit, R.S.	Kanpur			*			*										
1982d	Dixit, R.S.	Kanpur					*											
1982e	Dixit, R.S.	Kanpur					*											
1982	Dwivedi, S.	Eastern Plateau							*									
1982	Ghosh, M. and Mitra, G.N.	Bengal			*								*					
1982a	INDIA		*	*	*	*	*	*	*	*	*	*	*	*	*	*	*	*
1982b	INDIA		*	*	*	*	*	*	*	*	*	*	*	*	*	*	*	*
1982	Khandwe, M.A.	Amravati			*		*											

Year	Scholar	Study Area	Nature and Perspectives															
			1	2	3	4	5	6	7	8	9	10	11	12	13	14	15	16
1982	Mathur, R.S.	Jaipur									*			*				
1982	Nayak, H.P.	Uttar Pradesh			*									*				
1982	Ram, U. and Srivastava, V.K.	Ganga-Ghaghra Doab			*				*									
1982	Saxena, H.M.												*				*	
1982	Singh, L.R. and Dixit, R.S.	Kanpur					*											
1982	Singh, S.B.		*	*									*				*	*
1982	Swami, M.R.K., *et al.*		*												*			
1982	Wanmali, S., *et al.*																	*
1983a	Dixit, R.S.	Kanpur	*	*	*		*	*	*		*	*	*	*				
1983b	Dixit, R.S.	Kanpur			*													
1983c	Dixit, R.S.	Kanpur		*														
1983d	Dixit, R.S.	Kanpur		*														
1983e	Dixit, R.S.	Kanpur			*													
1983f	Dixit, R.S.	Kanpur																*
1983	Doshi, A.												*					
1983	Gedam, D.A.						*						*					
1983a	INDIA		*	*	*	*	*	*	*	*	*	*	*	*	*	*	*	*
1983b	INDIA		*	*	*	*	*	*	*	*	*	*	*	*	*	*	*	*
1983	Jamuna, K.	Madurai							*				*		*			
1983	Jogaiah, T.		*										*					
1983	Swaminathan, E. and Jothimai, P.	Udu Malpet											*	*	*		*	
1983	Krishan, G.	South India					*						*					
1983	Krishnamurthy, B.	Madurai											*			*		
1983	Kumaran, T.V.	Koppi Hills																*
1983	Lal, V.N. and Gupta, V.P.	Baberu			*													*

Year	Scholar	Study Area	Nature and Perspectives															
			1	2	3	4	5	6	7	8	9	10	11	12	13	14	15	16
1983	Murugesan,N.and Swaminathan,E.	Pudan Sandai										*	*		*			
1983	Nageshwari, S. and Gopalakrishnan, K.S.			*								*						
1983	Ramaswamy, G. and Shivamurthy, A.	Acharapakkam									*		*					
1983	Rao, M.S. and Kannan, M.	Tamil Nadu			*								*					
1983a	Saxena, H.M.	Rajasthan								*				*		*		
1983b	Saxena, H.M.	Rajasthan							*					*				
1983	Shantha Kumari A.	Trichy			*								*					
1983	Shivamurthy, A. and Ramaswamy, G.	Acharapakkam								*			*					
1983	Singh, L.R	India											*				*	
1983	Singh, L.R. and Lal, V.N.	Allahabad												*	*	*		*
1983	Singh, S.B. and Singh, B.N.											*						*
1983a	Srivastava, V.K.	Gorakhpur								*			*					
1983b	Srivastava, V.K.	North India											*					*
1983	Subbiah, S.	Trichurapally		*	*													*
1983a	Swaminathan, E.	Coimbatore and Madurai			*								*					
1983b	Swaminathan, E.	Madurai			*								*					
1983a	Tamaskar, B.G.		*	*								*		*				
1983b	Tamaskar, B.G.	Arvi Upland									*							
1983	Tamaskar, B.G. and Gedam, D.A.							*						*				
1983	Tripathi, V.S. and Chand, R.	Bulandshahr			*								*				*	
1984a	Dixit, R.S.	Kanpur			*													
1984b	Dixit, R.S.	Kanpur	*	*	*	*	*	*	*		*	*	*	*				*

Year	Scholar	Study Area	1	2	3	4	5	6	7	8	9	10	11	12	13	14	15	16
			Nature and Perspectives															
1984c	Dixit, R.S.	Bundelkhand									*	*						
1984d	Dixit, R.S.	Kanpur					*											
1984e	Dixit, R.S.	Kanpur				*												
1984f	Dixit, R.S.		*											*			*	
1984	Gedam, D.A.	Wardha Valley				*						*	*					
1984	INDIA		*	*	*	*	*	*	*	*	*	*	*	*	*	*	*	*
1984	Jamkar. A.G.	Dhule			*							*	*					
1984	Jayashankar, D.C.																	*
1984a	Kumbhar, A.P. & Deshmukh, P.W.	Sangli			*							*	*					
1984b	Kumbhar, A.P. & Deshmukh, P.W.	Sangli					*								*			
1984	Rao, K.V.S., *et al.*	Andhra Pradesh		*		*								*		*		
1984	Saharia, R.B. and Mathur, B.B.	Muradabad								*				*				
1984	Sharma, P.K. and Singh, D.K.	Central Assam			*			*										*
1984	Singh, L.R. and Sibou, S.	Allahabad								*				*				
1984	Singh, M.	Ganga-Ghaghara Doab											*		*			
1984	Srivastava, H.O.	Saryupar Plain										*						
1984	Srivastava, K.R. & Srivastava, V.K.	Tarai			*								*					
1984a	Srivastava, V.K.		*	*														*
1984b	Srivastava, V.K.	North India						*										
1984c	Srivastava, V.K.										*	*						
1984a	Subbiah, S.	Tamil Nadu	*	*														
1984b	Subbiah, S.	Tamil Nadu											*					*

Year	Scholar	Study Area	Nature and Perspectives															
			1	2	3	4	5	6	7	8	9	10	11	12	13	14	15	16
1984	Swaminathan, E. & Murugesan, N.	Pudan								*	*		*		*			
1984a	Tamaskar, B.G.					*							*					*
1984b	Tamaskar, B.G.		*															*
1984	Tiwari, R.C. and Tripathi, S.		*															*
1985	Alam. S.M., *et al.*	Hyderabad		*					*				*					
1985	De, N.K.																*	*
1985	Desai, G.M.	India												*			*	
1985a	Dixit, R.S.	Kanpur					*											
1985b	Dixit, R.S.	Hamirpur									*		*					
1985c	Dixit, R.S.	Kanpur	*	*	*		*	*	*			*	*	*				
1985d	Dixit, R.S.	Kanpur					*											
1985e	Dixit, R.S.	Hamirpur		*														
1985f	Dixit, R.S.	Hamirpur					*											
1985g	Dixit, R.S.	Hamirpur																*
1985h	Dixit, R.S.	Hamirpur						*										
1985	Dubey, R.S.	Madhya Pradesh														*		*
1985a	Gedam, D.A.	Wardha Valley										*						
1985b	Gedam, D.A.	Wardha Valley									*	*	*					
1985	Gopi, K.N., *et al.*	Hyderabad												*		*		
1985	Hugar, S.I.	Dharwad											*	*			*	
1985a	INDIA		*	*	*	*	*	*	*	*	*	*	*	*	*	*	*	*
1985b	INDIA		*	*	*	*	*	*	*	*	*	*	*	*	*	*	*	*
1985	Jamkar, A.G.	Dhule		*	*								*					
1985	Jodha, N.S.													*				*

Year	Scholar	Study Area	Nature and Perspectives															
			1	2	3	4	5	6	7	8	9	10	11	12	13	14	15	16
1985	Lal, H. and Yadav, H.R.	Gorakhpur												*			*	*
1985	Lal, V.N.	Bachhahawan											*	*				
1985	Kara	Paradip							*									*
1985	Katiyar, R.K.	Farrukhabad										*	*					
1985	Mandal, H.	Nagpur		*								*		*				
1985	Menon, K.P.A.													*				*
1985	Murthy, K.N., *et al.*	India									*			*				
1985	Nadkarni, M.V.			*										*				
1985	Nath, T. and Kushwaha, R.K.	Rampur Karkhana	*										*					
1985	Nath, V. and Nath, T.	Avadh Plain									*							
1985	Raju, V.T. and Bhatt, R.D.	Gujrat														*		*
1985	Rao, P.P.	India											*	*		*		
1985	Sikdar, B.P.		*											*				*
1985	Sharma, N.																	*
1985	Sharma, S.C.	Tarai		*												*		
1985	Shukla, S.K.	Sagar	*														*	*
1985	Singh, D.K. and Routray, R.K.												*				*	*
1985	Singh, L.R.	Uttar Pradesh			*									*			*	
1985	Sinha, B.R.K.	Patna											*					*
1985	Srivastava, H.O.	Saryupar Plain							*				*	*				
1985	Srivastava, R.C.	Bundelkhand			*													*
1985a	Srivastava, V.K.	Tarai									*		*					
1985b	Srivastava, V.K.																	*
1985	Subbarao, K.	India																*
1985	Sur, S.		*										*					

Year	Scholar	Study Area	Nature and Perspectives															
			1	2	3	4	5	6	7	8	9	10	11	12	13	14	15	16
1985	Surat, R.	Eastern, U.P.			*									*				
1985	Swaminathan, E.	Coimbatore			*			*										
1985a	Tamaskar, B.G.												*		*			
1985b	Tamaskar, B.G.	Arvi Upland			*													
1985	Tiwari, R.C. and Lal, N.	Rai Bareli											*				*	
1985	Twade, M.D. and Gophane, B.N.	Konkan														*		*
1985	Verma, S.C.	India	*											*				*
1985	Wanmali, S.	India			*								*			*		
1986a	Dixit, R.S.	Hamirpur			*													
1986b	Dixit, R.S.	Hamirpur							*									
1986c	Dixit, R.S.	Hamirpur										*	*					
1986d	Dixit, R.S.	Hamirpur										*	*					
1986e	Dixit, R.S.	Kanpur	*	*	*	*	*	*	*		*	*	*					
1986f	Dixit, R.S.		*															*
1986g	Dixit, R.S.		*														*	*
1986	Singh, L.R. and Dixit, R.S.	Kanpur	*					*	*								*	
1986	Jain, C.K. and Sharma, S.K.	Madhya Pradesh												*				
1986	Jana, M.M.	Silabati Basin			*								*					
1986	Tiwari, R.C. and Lal, V.N.	Rai Bareli			*								*					
1987a	Dixit, R.S.	Hamirpur			*													
1987b	Dixit, R.S.	Mahoba		*										*			*	
1987c	Dixit, R.S.	KAVAL Towns																*
1987d	Dixit, R.S.	Hamirpur			*								*					
1987e	Dixit, R.S.	Kanpur							*									
1987	Joshi, S.	Pune			*									*				*

Year	Scholar	Study Area	Nature and Perspectives															
			1	2	3	4	5	6	7	8	9	10	11	12	13	14	15	16
Further Additions:																		
1983	Arunachalam, B.																	*
1983	Chandran, K.	Shivaganga									*		*					
1983	Velayanathan, S.	Madurai									*		*					
1985	Rao, K.V.S., *et al.*	India	*	*									*	*				*
1985	Rao, P.P.	India			*								*	*				*
1985	Rao, TVS.& Subramaniyam, EVRS.			*	*										*			*
1985	Rao, HSG. and Maheshwari, A.													*				
1985	Saxena, H.M.	Rajasthan			*													

8 (II)

RESEARCH ARTICLES - I

THEMATIC TYPOLOGY - B

(Alphabetical Order)

ROLE

Agarwala, P.C. 1968. Aherwadkar, L.J. 1972. Andrade, C.P. 1972. Bedekar, S.L. 1972. Bhattacharya, B.N. 1973. Bhowmik, K.L. 1972. Das, T.K. 1975. Dixit, R.S. 1980aeg, 1981b, 1983a, 1984bf, 1985c, 1986efg. Gedam, D.A. 1981. INDIA, 1979, 1979, 1980, 1982ab, 1983ab, 1984, 1985ab. Jayaswal, S.N.P. 1963. Jogaiah, T. 1983. Kahlon, S.S. 1972. Kayastha, S.L. 1963. Kumar, S. 1980a. Lahiri, T.B. 1972. Lal, R.S. 1974. Mahalay, K.L. 1973. Mahato, S.N. 1974. Maikap, A.K, 1972. Malṣhe, P.T. 1979. Mathai, P.M. 1972. Narayanan, B.S. 1981. Nath, T. 1985. NCAER. 1982bc. Patel, A.M. 1963. Rao, K.V.S. 1985. Rao, T.V.S. 1985. Reddy, S.N. 1961. Sarkar, A.K. 1972. Sharma, S.K. 1980. Shukla, S.K. 1985. Sikder, B.P. 1985. Singh, H. 1965. Singh, J.P. 1980. Singh, K.N. 1961. Singh, L.R. 1986. Singh, S.B. 1982. Singh, S.K. 1972. Sinha, D.P. 1963. Sinha, S.N. 1961. Srivastava, V.K. 1977, 1980, 1984a. Subbiah, S. 1984. Sur, S. 1985. Swami, M.R.K. 1982. Tamaskar, B.G. 1983a, 1984b. Tiwari, R.C. 1984. Uppal, J.S. 1978. Vasudeo, Rao, D. 1980. Vepa, R.K. 1972. Verma, R.V. 1980. Verma, S.C. 1980, 1985. Wanmali, S. 1979, 1980.

ORIGIN/EVOLUTION

Agarwala, P.C. 1968. Aherwadkar, L.J. 1972. Alam, S.M. 1985. Andrade, C.P. 1972. Baruah, S.L. 1977. Bedekar, S.L. 1972. Bhagvati, A.K. 1978. Bhattacharya, B.N. 1973. Chakravarty, T. 1974. Das, M. 1968. Dayal, P. 1976. Deb, A.K. 1957. Dixit, R.S. 1980e, 1981j, 1983acd, 1984b, 1985ce, 1986e, 1987. Gedam, D.A. 1981. Ghosal, K. 1972. Gupta, S.K. 1967. INDIA. 1979, 1980, 1982ab, 1983ab, 1984, 1985ab. Jamkar, A.G. 1985. Jana, M.M. 1978. Janaki, V.K. 1962.

Jayashanker, D.C. 1976. Jayaswal, S.N.P. 1963. Kahlon, S.S. 1972. Kayastha, S.L. 1963. Kulkarni, K.M.1980. Lal, R.S. 1974. Mahalay, K.L. 1973. Mandal, H. 1985. Mukherjee, M. 1970. Nadkarni, M.V. 1985. Narayanan, B.S. 1981. NCAER 1971. Patel, A.M. 1963. Patil, B. 1975. Rao, B.P. 1969. Rao, K.V.S. 1984, 1985. Rao, T.V.S. 1985. Reddy, S.N. 1960. Sami, A. 1975ab, 1976, 1978. Sharma, S.C. 1985. Singh, H. 1965. Singh, K.N. 1960. Singh, S.B. 1982. Singh, S.K. 1972. Singh, S.M. 1965. Singh, U. 1959. Sinha, D.P. 1963. Sinha, S.N. 1960. Srivastava, K.R. 1974. Srivastava, V.K. 1977, 1980, 1984a. Subbiah, S. 1983, 1984. Suri, K.B. 1972. Tamaskar, B.G. 1977, 1978, 1979b, 1983a. Vepa, R.K. 1972. Verma, S.C. 1980. Vishwanath, M.S. 1972. Vishwanath, V.V. 1979. Wanmali, S. 1979.

LOCATION/DISTRIBUTION

Agarwala, P.C. 1968. Baruah, S.L. 1977. Bhattacharya, B.N. 1973. Bhowmik, K.L. 1972. Bose, N.K. 1949. Bose, P.K. 1982. Chatterjee, A.B. 1965. Das, M. 1968. De, J. 1979. Deb, A.K. 1957. Deshpande, C.D. 1941. Dixit, R.S. 1977, 1980e, 1981h, 1982c, 1983abc, 1984ab, 1985c, 1986ae, 1987ad. Ghosal, K. 1972. Ghosh, M. 1982. Gupta, N.L. 1972. Gupta, S.K. 1967. INDIA 1979, 1980, 1982ab, 1983ab, 1984, 1985ab. Jain, N.G. 1975. Jamkar, A.G. 1984, 1985. Jana, M.M. 1978, 1986. Joshi, S. 1987. Jayaswal, S.N.P. 1963. Kahlon, S.S. 1972. Kayastha, S.L. 1963. Khandwe, M.A. 1982. Krishan, G. 1963. Krishan, V. 1932, 1933, 1940. Kulkarni, G.S. 1963. Kulkarni, K.M. 1980. Kumbhar, A.P. 1984a. Lahiri, T.B. 1972. Lal, V.N. 1983. Mahato, S.N. 1974. Maikap, A.K. 1972. Mathai, P.M. 1972. Mohanty, P. 1972. Moharana, B.B. 1977. Mukherjee, A.B. 1957. Mukherjee, M. 1970. Mukherjee, S.P. 1968. Nageswari, S. 1983. Nayak, H.P. 1982. NCAER 1971, 1972a. Parvathi, C. 1975a, 1976. Patel, A.M. 1963. Paul, M.S. 1933. Ponnaiah, J.S. 1940. Prasad, A. 1978. Prasad, I. 1975. Ram, U. 1982. Raza, M. 1971. Ramakrishna, K.C. 1931. Ramakrishnan, N. 1969. Ramanandhan, V.V. 1955. Rao, B.P. 1966, 1967, 1969. Rao, M.S. 1983. Rao, P.P. 1985. Reddy, S.N. 1961. Saxena, H.M. 1972, 1985. Shafi, M. 1980. Shanthakumari, A. 1983. Sharma, B.D. 1976. Sharma, P.K. 1984. Sharma, R.C. 1981. Shasmal K.C. 1977. Singh, A.J. 1972. Singh, H. 1965. Singh, J. 1975. Singh, J.P. 1975. Singh, L.R. 1985. Singh, R.B. 1976. Singh, U. 1959, 1960. Sinha, D.P. 1963. Sinha, V.N.P. 1974. Sita, K. 1976. Srivastava, K.R. 1974, 1976, 1984. Srivastava, R.C. 1985. Srivastava, V.K. 1971, 1976a, 1977, 1979,

1980,1981. Subbiah, S. 1983. Surat, R. 1985. Suresh, R. 1971. Swaminathan, E. 1983ab, 1985. Tamaskar, B.G. 1966ab, 1978, 1979b, 1981, 1985. Thakur, B. 1968. Thyagarajan, V. 1940. Tiwari, R.C. 1986. Tripathi, V.S. 1983. Vasudeo, Rao, D. 1980. Venugopal, V. 1972. Verghese, I. 1971. Verma, L.N. 1968. Verma, R.V. 1980. Verma, S.C. 1980. Vishwanath, V.V.. 1979. Wanmali, S. 1976, 1985.

TRANSPORT NETWORK

Agarwal, B.C. 1978. Agarwala, P.C. 1968. Bedekar, S.L. 1972. Bhowmik, K.L. 1972. Bose, P.K. 1982. Chatterjee, A.B. 1969. Dixit, R.S. 1981cde, 1984be, 1986e. Gedam, D.A. 1984. INDIA 1979, 1980, 1982ab, 1983ab, 1984, 1985ab. Kulkarni, G.S. 1972. NCAER 1971. Prasad, I. 1975. Rao, B.P. 1969. Rao, K.V.S. 1984. Raza, M. 1980. Setharam, K. 1979. Tamaskar, B.G. 1966ab, 1979ac,1984a.

TYPOLOGY

Dixit, R.S. 1980be, 1981ag, 1982de, 1983a, 1984bd, 1985acdf, 1986e. Gedam, D.A. 1983. Ghosal, K. 1972. INDIA 1979, 1980, 1982ab,1983ab, 1984, 1985ab. Jana, M.M. 1978. Khandwe, M.A. 1982. Krishnan, G. 1983. Kumbhar, A.P. 1984b. Mukherjee, S.P. 1968. NCAER 1971. Singh, L.R. 1982. Srivastava, R.C. 1979. Srivastava, V.K. 1978, 1979. Tamaskar, B.G. 1966ab, 1983.

CENTRALITY/HIERARCHY

Baruah, S.L. 1977. Dixit, R.S. 1980ef, 1981b, 1982c, 1983a, 1984b, 1985ch, 1986e. Gedam, D.A. 1980. Ghoshal, K. 1972. Hall, K. 1977. Hashim, S.R. 1972. INDIA 1979, 1980, 1982ab, 1983ab, 1984, 1985ab. Jana, M.M. 1978. Katiyar, R.C. 1981. Kulkarni, G.S. 1972. Mukherjee, S.P. 1968. NCAER 1971. Setharan, K. 1979. Sharma, P.K. 1984. Singh, J. 1978. Singh, J.P. 1975. Singh, L.R. 1980, 1986. Sinha, V.N.P. 1974. Srivastava, H.D. 1980, 1985. Srivastava, V.K. 1976b, 1978, 1984b. Tamaskar, B.G. 1979b.

TRADE AREA

Agarwala, P.C. 1968. Agarwala, V.S. 1941. Alam, S.M. 1963, 1985. Chatterjee, A.B. 1965, 1969. Das, M. 1968. Dayal, P. 1976. Deb, A.K. 1957. Deshpande, C.D. 1941. Dixit, R.S. 1977, 1980e, 1982a,

1983a,1984b, 1985c, 1986bc, 1987c. Dutta, A.K. 1966ab, 1972a. Dwivedi, S. 1982. Gedam, D.A. 1974. Geetha, T. 1978. Ghosal, K. 1972. Gupta, N.L. 1972. Gupta, S.K. 1967. INDIA 1979, 1980, 1982ab, 1983ab, 1984, 1985ab. Jain, N.G. 1975. Jamuna, K. 1983. Jana, M.M. 1978. Janaki, V.K. 1962. Jayashankar, D.C. 1976. Jayaswal, S.N.P. 1963. Kara, 1985. Krishna, G. 1963. Kulkarni, G.S. 1963. Mahato, S.N. 1974. Mukherjee, A.B. 1955. Mukherjee, M. 1970. NCAER 1971. Parvathi, C. 1976. Ponnaiah, J.S. 1940. Prasad, I. 1975. Puja, H.G. 1938. Ram, U. 1982. Ramakrishna, K.C. 1931. Ramakrishnan, N. 1969. Ramamurthy, K. 1938. Ramanandhan, V.V. 1955. Rao, B.P. 1966, 1967. Raza, M. 1971. Sami, A. 1980a. Saxena, H.M. 1972, 1983b. Setharam, K. 1979. Sharma, B.D. 1976. Singh, H. 1965. Singh, L.R. 1986. Singh, U. 1959, 1960. Sinha, V.N.P. 1974. Srivastava, H.D. 1985. Srivastava, K.R. 1974. Srivastava,V.K. 1971. Tamaskar, B.G. 1978. Thakur, B. 1968. Verghese, I. 1971. Verma, R.V. 1980. Verma, S.C. 1980.

STRUCTURE/MORPHOLOGY

Alam, S.M. 1963. Baruah, S.L. 1977. Dayal, P. 1976. Dixit, R.S. 1980e. Gedam, D.A. 1974. INDIA 1979, 1980, 1982ab, 1983ab, 1984, 1985ab. Krishan, G. 1973. Kulkarni, K.M. 1980. Maidamwar, G.T. 1979. Malshe, P.T. 1979. Murugesan, 1983. NCAER 1971. Parvathi, C. 1975ab, 1976. Raza, M. 1971. Saharia, R.B. 1984. Sami, A. 1974, 1975a. Saxena, H.M. 1974, 1979, 1983a. Shivamurthy, A. 1983. Singh, J.P. 1975, 1980. Singh, K.N. 1961. Singh, L.R. 1984. Singh, R.L. 1977. Srivastava, K.R. 1974. Srivastava, V.K. 1983a. Swaminathan, E. 1984. Venugopal, V. 1972. Verma, L.N. 1968.

CONSUMER/TRADER BEHAVIOUR

Chandran, K. 1980, 1983. Chatterjee, A.B. 1969. Dixit, R.S. 1980e, 1983a, 1984bc, 1985b, 1986e. Dutta, A.K. 1966ab, 1972ab. Gedam, D.A. 1974, 1985. INDIA 1979, 1980, 1982ab, 1983ab, 1984, 1985ab. Jothimai, P. 1983. Kumar, S. 1980b. Mathur, R.S. 1982. Murthy, K.N. 1985. Murugesan, N. 1983. Nath, V. 1985. NCAER 1971. Ramaswami, G. 1983. Saxena, H.M. 1980a. Singh, J. 1978. Srivastava, R.C. 1979. Srivastava, V.K. 1978, 1984c, 1985. Swaminathan, E. 1984. Tamaskar, B.G. 1970, 1983b. Thakur, B. 1974. Velaynathan, S. 1983.

SYNCHRONIZATION/CYCLES/RINGS

Chandran, K. 1980. Dixit, R.S. 1980ceh, 1981fij, 1982b, 1983a, 1984bc, 1985c, 1986cee. Gedam, D.A. 1985. INDIA 1979, 1980, 1982ab, 1983ab, 1984, 1985ab. Jamkar, A.G. 1984. Jothimai, P. 1983. Katiyar, R.K. 1985. Kumbhar, A.P. 1984a. Mandal, H. 1985. NCAER 1971. Singh, S.B. 1983. Srivastava, H.O. 1984. Srivastava, R.C. 1979. Srivastava, V.K. 1977, 1978, 1984c. Tamaskar, B.G. 1978, 1979b, 1983a. Verma, R.V. 1980. Verma, S.C. 1980.

TRADITIONAL EXCHANGE/PERIODIC MARKETING

Agarwala, P.C. 1968. Alam, S.M. 1985. Banrod, R.G. 1977. Chandra, R. 1973. Chandran, K. 1980, 1983. Deshpande, C.D. 1941. Dixit, R.S. 1980e, 1981j, 1983a, 1984b, 1985ab, 1986cde, 1987d. Doshi A. 1983. Gedam D.A. 1974. 1981, 1983, 1984, 1985. Geetha, T. 1978. Ghosh, M. 1982. Hugar, S.I. 1985. INDIA. 1979, 1980, 1982ab, 1983ab, 1984, 1985ab. Jain, N.G. 1975. Jamkar, A.G. 1984, 1985. Jamuna, K. 1983. Jana, M.M. 1986. Jogaiah, T. 1983. Jothimai, P. 1983. Katiyar, R.C. 1985. Khan, W. 1972. Krishan, G. 1983. Krishnamurthy, B. 1983. Krishnan, V. 1932, 1933, 1940. Kumbhar, A.P. 1984a. Maidamvar, G.T. 1979. Malshe, P.T. 1979. Mathai, P.M. 1972. Mathur, V.S. 1941. Metra, I. 1980. Moharana, B.B. 1977. Mukherjee, A.B. 1957. Murugesan, N. 1983. Nageswari, S. 1983. Nath, T. 1985. Nath, V. 1981. NCAER 1971. Parvathi, C. 1976. Patel, A.M. 1963. Pattanaik, N. 1953. Paul, M.S. 1933. Ponnaiah, J.S. 1940. Ramakrishnan, N. 1969. Ramaswami, G. 1983. Rao, M.S. 1983. Rao, P.P. 1985. Raza, M. 1971. Saxena, H.M. 1972, 1982, 1985. Shamsal, K.C. 1977. Shanthakumari, A. 1983. Shivamurthi, A. 1983. Singh, D.K. 1985. Singh, J. 1978. Singh, L.R. 1983. Singh, M. 1984. Singh, R.L. 1977. Singh, S.B. 1982. Singh, U. 1959. Singhal, R.C. 1979. Sinha, B.R.K. 1985. Sinha, S. 1951. Sinha, S.N. 1961. Sita, K. 1976. Srivastava, H.O. 1985. Srivastava, K.R. 1974, 1976, 1984. Srivastava, R.C. 1979. Srivastava, V.K. 1978, 1979,1983ab, 1985. Subbiah, S. 1984. Sur, S. 1985. Suresh, R. 1971. Swami, M.R.K. 1982. Swami, P. 1942. Swaminathan, E. 1983ab, 1984. Tamaskar, B.G. 1955, 1965. Tamaskar, B.G. 1966ab, 1977, 1978, 1979abc, 1983, 1984a, 1985. Tiwari, R.C. 1985, 1986. Tripathi, V.S. 1983. Uppal, J.S. 1979. Vasudeo Rao, D. 1980. Velaynathan, S. 1983. Verghese, I. 1971. Verma, L.N. 1968. Verma, R.V. 1980. Vishwanath, V.V. 1979. Wanmali, S. 1979, 1980, 1985.

URBAN/DAILY/REGULATED/AGRICULTURAL

Aherwadkar, L.J. 1972. Alam, S.M. 1963. Andrade, C.P. 1972. Bumb, B.L. 1972. Chatterjee, A.B. 1965. Dayal, P. 1976. Desai, G.M. 1985. Dixit, R.S. 1980e, 1983a, 1984bf, 1985c, 1987b. Duggal, S.L. 1974. Dutta, A.K. 1966ab, 1972a. Garg, P.K. 1972ab. Gopi, K.N. 1985. Hugar, S.I. 1985. INDIA 1979, 1980, 1982ab, 1983ab, 1984, 1985ab. Jain, C.K. 1986. Jain, N.G. 1975. Jodha, N.S. 1985. joshi, S. 1987. Kala, S.C. 1976. Krishan, G. 1973. Kulkarni, K.M. 1980. Lal, H. 1985. Lal, V.N. 1985. Mandal, H. 1985. Mani, K.C. 1981. Mathai, P.M. 1972. Mathur, R.S. 1982. Mathur, V.S. 1941. Menon, K.P.A. 1985. Mohanty, P. 1982. Murthy, K.N. 1985. Muthiah, C. 1972. Nadkarni, M.V. 1985. Narayanan, B.S. 1981. Nayak, H.P. 1982. NCAER 1971. Patil, B. 1975. Ponnaiah, J.S. 1940. Prasad, A. 1978. Rao, H.S.G. 1985. Rao, K.V.S. 1984, 1985. Rao, P.P. 1985. Rao, T.V.S. 1985. Raza, M. 1980. Saharia, R.B. 1984. Sami, A. 1974, 1975a, 1976, 1978, 1980a. Saxena, H.M. 1980a, 1983ab. Sikaer, B.P. 1985. Singh, A.J. 1972. Singh, J. 1975. Singh, K.N. 1960. Singh, L.R. 1983, 1984. Srivastava, H.O. 1985. Srivastava, K.R. 1974. Srivastava, R.C. 1979. Srivastava, V.K. 1981. Surat, R. 1985. Tamaskar, B.G. 1983a. Thakur, B. 1974. Uppal, J.S. 1978. Veeranna, S. 1963. Verghese, I. 1971. Verma, S.C. 1985. Vishwanath, M.S. 1972. Wanmali, S. 1979, 1980.

FUNCTION

Agarwala, V.S. 1941. Alam, S.N. 1963. Chakravarty, T. 1974. Dayal P. 1976. Dixit RS 1977, 1980c. Dutta AK 1972a. Garg PK 1972b. Gupta NL 1972. Hashim SR 1972. INDIA 1979, 1980. 1982ab. 1983ab, 1984, 1985ab. Jamuna K 1983. Jothimai P 1983. Kumar A 1977. Kumbhar AP 1984b. Mahato SN 1974. Mukherjee M 1970. Mukherjee SP 1968. NCAER 1971. Ramakrishnan N 1969. Rao BP 1967. Raza M 1971. Sami A 1975b, 1978. Sharma BD 1976. Singh H 1965. Singh KN 1961. Singh LR 1983. Singh M 1984. Singh RB 1976. Singh U 1960. Srivastava VK 1971. Swaminathan E 1984. Tamaskar BG 1985. Thakur B 1968.

GOODS/COMMODITIES

Agarwal VS 1941. Bose NK 1949. Bose PK 1982. Chakravarty T

1974. Chatterjee AB 1969. Das M 1968. De J 1979. Deb AK 1957. Dixit RS 1980e. Dubey RS 1985. Gopi KN 1985. Gupta NL 1972. Gupta SK 1967. INDIA 1979, 1980, 1982ab. 1983ab. 1984, 1985ab. Krishan G 1963. Krishnamurthy B. 1983. Mahato SN 1974. Maikap AK 1972. Mukherjee AB 1955. Mukherjee M 1970. NCAER 1971. Paul MS 1933. Ponnaiah JS 1940, Punja HG 1938. Raju VT 1985. Ramakrishna KC 1931, 1939. Ramakrishnan N 1969. Ramamurthy, K. 1938. Rämanandham VV 1955. BP 7, 1969. Rao KVS 1984. Rao PP 1985. Rao RS 1966. Rao TVS 1985. Raza M 1980. Reddy SN 1961. Saxena HM 1983a. Setharam K 1979. Safi M 1980. Sharma BD 1976. Sharma SC 1985. Singh H 1965. Singh J 2974. Singh KN 1961. Singh LR 1983. Singh RB 1976. Singh U 1959, 1960. Thakur B 1968. Thyagarajan V 1940. Twade MD 1985. Vishwanath VV 1979. Wanmali S 1976, 1985.

PLANNING

Bawa RL 1972. Bhat LS 1972. Bhawmik KL 1972. Bedekar SL 1972. Bose AN 1972. Das PK 1975. De NK 1985. Desai GM 1985. Dixit RS 1980eg, 1984f, 1986g, 197b. Gupta PK 1972ab. Gupta VK 1972. Hugar SI 1985. INDIA 1979, 1980, 1982ab, 1983ab, 1984, 1985ab. Jain NG 1975. Jayashankar DC 1979. Kahlon SS 1972. Maikap AP 1972. Mathai PM 1972. Mathur GC 1972. Muthaih C 1972. Negeswari S. 1983. NCAER 1971, 1972abcd. Pattil B 1975. Rao PP 1972. Reddy NV 1972. Sarkar AK 1972. Saxena HM 1982. Selvam LG 1972. Shaha SM 1972. Sharma SK 1980. Shukla SK 1985. Singh DK 1985. Singh LR 1983, 1985, 1986. Singh SB 1982. Singh SK 1972. Singhal RC 1979. Talwar BR 1972. Tamakar BG 1966a. Tiwari RG 1985. Tripathi VS 1983. Uppal JS 1979. Vasudeo Rao D 1980. Vishwanath MS 1972. Wanmali S 1979, 1980.

OTHERS
[1]

Agarwal BC 1978. Aiyasami U 1981. Anjea RK 1978. Arunachalam B 1983. Banrod RG 1977. Bhagbati AK 1978. Bose PK 1982. Chandra R 1973. Das PK 1974. Das TK 1975. De J 1979. De NK 1985. Deb AK 1957. Dixit RS 1980ade, 1983f. 1984b. 1985b. 1986fh. 1987c. Dubey

1. *Note* : Details are given in the Bibliography.

RS 1985. Ghosal K 1972. Hall K 1977. INDIA 1979, 1980, 1982ab, 1983ab, 1984. Jodha NS 1985. Joshi S 1987. Kala Sc 1976. Kara 1985. Katiyar RC 1981. Kayastha SL 1963. Kulkarni GS 1972. Kumar A 1977. Sumar S 1980a. Labiri TB 1972. Lal H 1985. Lal RS 1974. Lal VN 1983. Mahaley KL 1973. Maidamwar GT 1979. Malshe PT 1979. Mani KC 1981 Menon KPA 1985. Mohanty SK 1980. Moharana BB 1977. Mukherjee AB 1955. NCAER 1971. Patil B 1975. Paul MS 1933. Raju VT 1985. Ramamurthy K 1938. Ramanandhan VV 1955. Rao BP 1967, 1969. Rao KVS 1985. Rao PP 1985. Rao RB 1966. Sami A 1975b, 1976, 1980b. Saxena HM 1977, 1979, 1980b. Setharam K 1979. Shafi M. 1972. Sharma BD 1976. Sharma N 1985. Sharma PK 1984. Sharma RC 1981. Shasmal KC 1977. Shukla SK 1985. Sikder BP 1985. Singh A 1967. Singh DK 1985. Singh J 1979. Singh JP 1980. Singh LR 1980, 1983, 1985. Singh RB 1976. Singh RL 1977. Singh SB 1982, 1983. Singhal RC 1979. Sinha BRK 1985. Srivastava HO 1980. Srivastava KR 1974, 1984. Srivastava RC 1985. Srivastava VK 1976ab, 1978, 1983b, 1984a, 1985b. Subbarao K 185. Subbish S 1983, 1984. Tamaskar BG 1977, 1979ac, 1981, 1984ab, 1985. Thyagarajan V 1940. Tiwari RC 1984. Twade MD 1985. Uppal JS 1979. Verma SC 1980, 1985. Vishwanath VV 1979. Wanmali S 1982.

9

RESEARCH ARTICLES - II

OTHERS ON INDIAN PERSPECTIVES

(Alphabetical Order)

Armstrong, C.G. (1930). Madras Harbour, *Journal of Madras Geographical Association*, 5(1).

Armstrong, C.G. (1939). Ports of Madras, *Journal of Madras Geographical Association*, 14(2).

Ash, W.C. (1933). Vishakhapatnam Harbour, *Journal of Madras Geographical Association*, 8(1).

Astor, A. (1982). Bazaar - A cultural and structural study, *Man in India*, 62(1), 19-61.

Beatty, G.F. (1982). Marketing of fresh vegetables and fruits in Calcutta, *Geographical Review of India*, 44(1).

Bohle, H.G. (1981a). Diversity in commodity flow in a south Indian weekly market system : Spatio-temporal patterns and functional implications, *The Deccan Geographer*, 19(1), 1-18.

Bohle, H.G. (1981b). Spatio-temporal decision making in south Indian weekly markets : An investigation into consumer-trader perceptions and preferences, *The National Geographical Journal of India*, 27(1-2), 1-13.

Bohle, H.G. (1985). Mobile trade in South India, *Proceedings International Conference*, Geography Department, Gorakhpur University Dec.

Bradnock, R.W. (1974). The hinterlands of Bangalore, and Madras, *The Indian Geographical Journal*, 49(1).

Fox, R.G. (1967). Family, caste and commerce in a north Indian market town, *Economic Development and Regional Change*, 15, 297-314.

Fox, R.G. (1979). Influence of periodic markets on the occupational structure of rural settlements, *The Deccan Geographer*, 17(1), 555-558.

Harriss, B. (1975). Poverty, caste, rurality of transactions: A speculative explanation for periodic marketing in northern Tamil Nadu, *Proceedings - Second Indo-British Seminar*, Cambridge.

Harriss, B. (1976). Social specificity in rural weekly market - The case of northern Tamil Nadu, India, *Proceedings International Geographical Union Working Group on Market Distribution Systems*, 23rd International Geography Congress, Moscow.

Harriss, B. (1979). State intervention of dryland foodgrain markets and price inequality in Andhra Pradesh and Karnatak States, *Proceedings - Third Indo-British Geography Seminar.*

Harriss, B. (1980a). Regulated foodgrains markets : A critique, *Social Scientist, India*, 9(2), 22-31.

Harriss, B. (1980b). Inaction, interaction, and action - Regulated agricultural markets in Tamil Nadu, *Social Scientist, India*, 9(4), 96-137.

Harriss, B. (1981). The distribution of agricultural mercantile power in Tamil Nadu, *Transactions: Centre for Regional Ecological and Science Studies in Development Alternatives*, 1, 19-28.

Harriss, B. (1983a). Relations of production and exchange and poverty in rain-fed agricultural regions, *Economic and Political Weekly*, 18, 24/9/83, 82-92.

Harriss, B. (1983b). Implication of food distribution policies - A case study in south India, *Food Policy*, 121-30.

Harriss, B. (1985). Agricultural markets and inter-sectoral resource transfers: Cases from the Semi-Arid Tropics of South-East Asia, in *Agricultural Markets in the Semi-Arid Tropics*, Patancheru, International Crop Research Institute for the Semi-Arid Tropics, 279-304.

Hirt, H.F. (1975). The oriental bazaar - A case study for India, *The Indian Geographical Journal*, 50(1), 13-25.

Johnson, E.A.J. (1972). The integration of agrarian, commercial and industrial activities in functional economic areas, in *Market Towns and Spatial Development*, New Delhi, National Council of Applied Economic Research, 57-76.

Joseph, S.E. (1972). Industrial dispersal in India, in *Market Towns and Spatial Development*, New Delhi, National Council of Applied Economic Research, 121-24.

Master, M.A. (1953). Problems facing Indian shipping, *Andhra Chamber of Commerce, Silver Jubilee Volume 1.*

Miltendorf, H.J. (1982). Rural market centre - Potential development centre for small farmer development, *Indian Journal of Public*

Administration, 28(1), 101-19.

Neale, W. *et al.* (1965). Kurali market - A report on the economic geography of marketing in northern Punjab, *Economic Development and Cultural Change*, 13, 129-68.

Warrior, S.K. (1972). Some problems of a public marketing agency and their impact on the marketing development programme, in *Market Towns and Spatial Development*, New Delhi, National Council of Applied Economic Research, 75-78.

10

RESEARCH CONTRIBUTIONS – CLASSIFIED

(Alphabetical Order)

Agarwala, B.C.	P(1978).
Agarwala, P.C.	P(1968).
Agarwala, V.S.	P(1941).
Aherwadjar, L.J.	P(1972).
Aiyasami, U.	P(1981).
Alam, S.M.	P(1963, 1985).
Andrade, C.P. and Johnson, A.A.	P(1972).
Aneja, R.K.	P(1978).
Armstrong, C.G.	P(1930, 1939).
Arunachalam, B.	A(1983).
Ash, W.C.	P(1933).
Astor, A.	P(1982).
Banrod, R.G.	P(1977).
Barnum, H.	PR(1964, Ph.D.).
Barunu, H.	BM(1956).
Baruah, S.L.	P(1977).
Bawa, R.L.	P(1972).
Beatty, G.F.	P(1982).
Bedekar, S.L.	P(1972).
Bentley, O.A.	BM(1929).
Bhagvati, A.K.	P(1978).
Bhat, L.S.	P(1972).
Bhattacharya, B.N.	P(1973).
Bhowmik, K.L. and Chaudhary, K.K.	P(1972).

Abbreviations: BM = Book/Monograph, PR = Project Report, P = Paper, and A = Abstract.

Bohle, H.G.	P(1981ab), A(1985).
Bose, A.N.	P(1972).
Bose, N.K.	P(1949).
Bose, P.K.	P(1982).
Bradnock, R.W.	P(1974).
Bumb, B.L.	P(1972).
Chakravarty, T.	A(1974).
Chandra, R.	P(1973).
Chandran, K.	PR(1978, M. Phil.), A(1980, 1983).
Chatterjee, A.B.	P(1965, 1969).
Chaudhary, S.	BM(1975).
CONCEPT	BM(1982).
Das, M.	A(1968).
Das, P.K.	A(1974).
Das, T.K.	P(1975).
Dayal, P. and Thakur, B.	P(1976).
De, J.	P(1979).
De, N.K.	A(1985).
Deb, A.K.	P(1957).
Desai, G.M.	P(1985).
Deshpande, C.D.	P(1941).
Dixit, R.S.	BM(1979b, 1984g), PR(1979a, D. Phil., 1984h, ICSSR) P(1977, 1980degh, 1981e, 1982cde, 1983befg, 1984abcde, 1985bdefg, 1986bcdefg, 1987de), A(1980abef, 1981abcdfghij, 1982ab, 1983acd, 1984f, 1985ach, 1986a, 1987abc).
Doshi, A.	P(1983).
Dubey, R.S.	A(1985).
Duggal, S.L.	P(1974).
Dutta, A.K.	P(1966ab, 1972).
Dutta, A.K. and Harrity, P.B.	P(1972).
Dwivedi, S.	P(1982).

Fox, R.G.	P(1967, 1979).
Garg, P.K.	P(1972ab).
Gedam, D.A.	PR(1978, Ph. D.), P(1974, 1980, 1981, 1983, 1984, 1985a), A(1985b).
Geetha, T.	PR(1977, M. Phil.), P(1978).
Ghosal, K.	P(1972).
Ghosh, M. and Mitra, G.	P(1982).
Gopi, K.N. and Dunkerley, J.	P(1985).
Gormsen, E.	BM(1985).
Gupta, N.L. and Hiren, S.	P(1972).
Gupta, S.K.	P(1967).
Gupta, V.K.	P(1972).
Hall, K.	P(1977).
Harriss, B.	BM(1981a, 1984ab), P(1976, 1980ab, 1981b, 1983ab, 1985), A(1975, 1979).
Hashim, S.R.	P(1972).
Hirt, H.F.	P(1975).
Hugar, S.I.	PR(1984, Ph. D.), A(1985).
Hussain, S.A.	BM(1937).
ICRISAT	BM(1985).
ICSSR	BM(1972, 1975, 1976, 1977, 1978, 1979, 1980, 1981, 1982, 1984).
IGU	BM(1972 - 1985, eds. R.H.T. Smith/E. Gormsen), (1986 - 1987, eds. A. Metton/C. Nordin).
INDIA	BM(Undated), A(1979, 1980, 1982ab, 1983ab, 1984, 1985ab).
Ishihara, H.	BM(1961, 1978, 1979, 1983ab, 1985ab).
Jain, C.K. and Sharma, S.K.	P(1986).
Jain, N.G.	P(1975).
Jamkar, A.G.	P(1984), A(1985).

Leon, S.	BM(1979).
Mahalanobis, J.N.	P(1972).
Mahalay, K.L.	P(1973).
Mahato, S.N.	P(1974).
Maidamvar, G.T.	PR(1979, Ph. D.), P(1979a).
Maikap, A.K.	P(1972).
Malshe, P.T.	P(1979).
Mandal, H.	P(1985).
Mani, K.C.	P(1981).
Master, M.A.	P(1953).
Mathai, P.M.	P(1972).
Mathur, G.C.	P(1972).
Mathur, R.S.	P(1982).
Mathur, V.S.	P(1941).
Mehtra, I.	P(1980).
Menon, K.P.A.	P(1985).
Metton, A.	BM(1986ab, 1987 same as IGU)
Miltendorf, H.J.	P(1982).
Mitra, A.	BM(1953).
Mohanty, P.	P(1972).
Mohanty, S.K.	PR(1980, Ph. D.).
Mohanty, S.K. and Singh, D.K.	P(1980).
Moharana, B.B.	P(1970).
Mukherjee, A.P.	P(1955, 1957).
Mukherjee, M.	P(1970).
Mukherjee, S.P.	P(1968).
Murthy, K.N. and Oppen von M.	P(1985)
Murugesan, N. and Swaminathan, E.	A(1983).
Muthiah, C.	P(1972).
Nadkarni, M.V.	P(1985).
Nageswari, S. and Gopalkrishan, K.S.	A(1983).
Narayan, B.S.	P(1981).
Nath, T. and Kushwaha, R.K.	A(1985).
Nath, V.	PR(1983, Ph. D.).
Nath, V. and Jain, A.K.	P(1981).
Nath, V. and Nath, T.	A(1985).
Nayak, H.P.	P(1982).

Rao, T.V.S. and Subramanium, E.V.	P(1985).
Rathore, N.S.	PR(1979, Ph. D.).
Raza, M.	BM(1979 same as ICSSR), P(1971, 1979, 1980).
Reddy, N.V.	P(1972).
Reddy, S.N.	P(1961).
Sami, A.	PR(1975, Ph. D.), P(1974, 1975ab, 1976, 1978, 1980ab), BM(1980c).
Saharia, R.B. and Mathur, B.B.	P(1984).
Sarkar, A.K.	P(1972).
Saxena, H.M.	BM(1975, 1984), PR(1971, Ph. D., 1980c, ICSSR), P(1972, 1974, 1977, 1979, 1980b, 1982, 1983ab), A(1980a, 1985).
Selvam, L.G.	P(1972).
Setharam, K.	P(1979).
Shafi, M.	P(1972, 1980).
Shah, S.M.	P(1972).
Shantha Kumari, A.	A(1983).
Sharma, B.D.	P(1976).
Sharma, N.	A(1985).
Sharma, P.K.	PR(1983, Ph. D.).
Sharma, P.K. and Singh, D.K.	P(1984).
Sharma, R.C. and Kumar, A.	P(1981).
Sharma, S.C.	A(1985).
Sharma, S.K. and Archana	P(1980).
Shasmal, K.C.	P(1977).
Shukla, S.K.	A(1985).
Sikder, B.P	P(1985).
Singh, A.	P(1967).
Singh, A.J.	P(1972).
Singh, D.K. and Routray, R.K.	A(1985).
Singh, H.	P(1965).
Singh, J.	P(1975, 1979).
Singh, J.P.	P(1975, 1980).
Singh, K.N.	PR(1962, Ph. D.), P(1961).
Singh, L.R.	P(1980a, 1982, 1983ab, 1984, 1986), A(1980bc, 1985).

Singh, M.	P(1984).
Singh, R.B. and Singh, K.K.	P(1976).
Singh, R.L. and Singh, R.P.B.	P(1977).
Singh, S.B.	P(1982).
Singh, S.B. and Singh, B.N.	P(1983).
Singh, S.K.	P(1972).
Singh, S.M.	PR(1958 M.A.), P(1965).
Singh, U.	P(1959, 1960).
Singhal, R.C.	P(1979).
Sinha, B.N.	BM(1974, 1983, 1984, 1986).
Sinha, B.R.K.	A(1985).
Sinha, D.P.	BM(1968), PR(1964, Ph. D.), P(1963).
Sinha, M.K.	PR(1968, M.C.P.).
Sinha, S.	P(1951, 1961).
Sinha, V.N.P. and Mandal, R.B.	P(1974).
Sita, K.	P(1976).
Sivamurthy, A. and Ramaswamy, G.	A(1983).
Srivastava, H.O.	PR(1980, Ph. D.), P(1984), A(1985).
Srivastava, H.O. and Srivastava, B.K.	P(1984).
Srivastava, K.R.	PR(1983, Ph. D.), P(1974, 1976).
Srivastava, K.R. and Srivastava, V.K.	P(1984).
Srivastava, R.C.	A(1985).
Srivastava, R.C. and Gupta, J.P.	P(1979).
Srivastava, V.K.	BM(1983, 1984d, 1987), PR(1982, ICSSR), P(1971, 1976ab, 1977, 1978ab, 1979, 1980, 1981, 1983ab, 1984ab, 1985), A(1984c, 1985b).
Subbarao, K.	P(1985).
Subbiah, S.	A(1983, 1984).
Sur, S.	P(1985).
Surat, R.	A(1985).
Suresh, R.	P(1971).
Suri, K.B.	P(1972).
Swami, M.R.K. *et al.*	P(1982).
Swami, P.	P(1942).
Swaminathan, E.	PR(1977, Ph. D.), A(1983ab,

	1985).
Swaminathan, E. and Murugesan, N.	P(1984).
Talwar, B.R.	P(1972).
Tamaskar, B.G.	PR(1979d), P(1955, 1965, 1966ab, 1977, 1978, 1979abc, 1981, 1983ab, 1984ab; 1985a), A(1985b).
Thakur, B.	P(1974), A(1968).
Thyagarajan, V.	P(1940).
Tiwari, R.C. and Lal, V.N.	P(1986), A(1985).
Tiwari, R.C. and Tripathi, S.	P(1984).
Tripathi, V.B. and Chand, R.	P(1983).
Twade, M.D. and Gophane, B.W.	A(1985).
Uppal, J.S.	P(1978, 1979).
Vasudeo Rao, D.	P(1980).
Veeranna, S.	P(1963).
Velaynathan, S.	A(1983)
Venugopal, V.	A(1972).
Vepa, R.K.	P(1972).
Verghese, I.	P(1971).
Verma, L.N. and Saxena, H.M.	P(1968).
Verma, R.D.	PR(1987, Ph. D.).
Verma, R.V.	P(1980).
Verma, S.C.	P(1980, 1985).
Vishwanath, M.S.	PR(1966, Ph. D.), P(1972).
Vishwanath, V.V.	PR(1979b, Ph. D.), P(1979a).
Wanmali, S.	BM(1980 - 1981), PR(1978, Ph. D., 1983), P(1976, 1980, 1985), A(1979).
Wanmali, S. *et al.*	A(1982).
Warrior, S.K.	P(1972).

11

BIBLIOGRAPHY

(Alphabetical Order)

Agarwala, B.C. (1978) Economic networks and cultural integration in M.P., *Man in India*, 58(4), 285-97.

Agarwala, P.C. (1968) Weekly market size and service area in Bastar district, M.P., *The Indian Geographical Journal*, 43(1-4), 29-33.

Agarwala, V.S. (1941) Trade and commerce from Panini's Ashtaadhyayi, *Transactions Indian History Congress*, V Session, 134-41.

Aherwadkar, L.J. (1972) Role of regulated marketing in the development of market centres - A case study of Marathawada, in *Market Towns and Spatial Development*, New Delhi, Indian Council of Applied Economic Research, 187-91.

Aiyasami, U. and Bohle, H.G. (1981) Market access as constraint on marginal and small farmers, *Economic and Political Weekly*, 16(13), March 28.

Alam, S.M. (1963) Commercial structure of the cities of Hyderabad and Secunderabad, *Journal of the Osmania University: Arts, Commerce, Law and Education*, 1, 1-10.

Alam, S.M., Mookherjee, M. and Singh, D. (1985) Periodic markets as growth centres in the rural hinterland of metropolitan Hyderabad, in *Agricultural Markets in the Semi-Arid Tropics*, Patancheru, International Crop Research Institute for the Semi-Arid Tropics, 139-46.

Andrade, C.P. and Johnson, A.A. (1972) The role of market centres and regulated marketing in the development process - The Khanna example, in *Market Towns and Spatial Development*, New Delhi, National Council of Applied Economic Research, 160-65.

Aneja, R.K. (1978) New demand for 'Sheri Saman', *Times of India*, March 6, 8.

Armstrong, C.G. (1930) Madras Harbour, *Journal of Madras Geographical Association*, 5(1).

Armstrong, C.G. (1939) Ports of Madras, *Journal of Madras*

Geographical Association, 14(2).

Arunachalam, B. (1983) The Geography of rural markets in India - An inventory and prospect, *Proceedings of All-Inddia Symposium on the Impact of Weekly Markets on Rural Societies*, Geography Department, Madurai University, October 7-10.

Ash, W.C. (1933) Vizagapatnam harbour, *Journal of Madras Geographical Association*, 8(1).

Astor, A. (1982) Bazaar - A cultural and structural study, *Man in India*, 6(1), 19-61.

Banrod, R.G. (1977) Shandies of the village weekly market, *Administrator*, 22, 399-401.

Barnum, H. (1964) *A Model of the Markets for Foodgrains in India*, Ph.D. Dissertation, Berkley, University of California.

Barunu, H. and Baneja, J.D. (1956) *The Fairs and Festivals of Assám*, Gauhati, D.N. Dutta.

Baruah, S.L. (1977) Market system in Assam during the days of Ahoms, *Assam Economic Journal*, 3(1), 62-72.

Bawa, R.L. *et al.* (1972) Market towns and spatial development - A case study of north Bihar, in *Market Towns and Spatial Development*, New Delhi, National Council of Applied Economic Research, 179-82.

Beatty, G.F. (1982) Marketing of fresh vegetables and fruits in Calcutta, *Geographical Review of India*, 44(1).

Bedekar, S.L. (1972) Role of regulated markets in the development of rural areas, in *Market Towns and Spatial Development*, New Delhi, National Council of Applied Economic Research, 99-102.

Bentley, O.A. (1929) *Fairs and Festivals in Bengal*.

Bhagbati, A.K. (1978) A geographical note on Kaithalkunchi with special referance to the growth of its market centre, *The Journal of North-East India Geographical Society*, 10(1-2).

Bhat, L.S. (1972)/ Regional planning in India - A suggested model, in *Market Towns and Spatial Development*, New Delhi, Indian council of Applied Economic Research, 89-92.

Bhattacharya, B.N. (1973) Geography of market places - A case study of north Bengal, *The Journal of North-East India Geographical Society*, 5(1-2).

Bhowmik, K.L. and Chaudhary, K.K. (1972) Rural markets and system of mass communication, in *Market Towns and Spatial Development*, New Delhi, Indian Council of Applied Economic Research, 139-41.

Bradnock, R.W. (1974) The hinterlands of Bangalore and Madras, *The Indian Geographical Journal*, 49 (1).

Bohle, H.G. (1981a) Diversity in commodity flow in a south Indian weekly market system : Spatio-temporal patterns and functional implications, *The Deccan Geographer*, 19(1), 1-18.

Bohle, H.G. (1981b) Spatio-temporal decision making in south Indian weekly markets : An investigation into consumer-trader perceptions and preferences, *The National Geographical Journal of India*, 27(1-2), 1-13.

Bohle, H.G. (1985) Mobile trade in rural south India - From the perspective development theory, *Proceedings of International Coference on Commerical Activities and Rural Development*, Geography Department, Gorakhpur University, December 2 *International Conference: Commerical Activities and Rural Development*, Department of Geography, Gorakhpur University, December 23-25.

Bose, A.N. (1972) Socio-economic basis of small town development, in *Market Towns and Spatial Development*, New Delhi, National Council of Applied Economic Research, 142-44.

Bose, N.K. (1949) Partition and trade, *Calcutta Geographical Review*, 11(1).

Bose, P.K. (1982) Production organisation and market relations of potters of Gujrat, *Man in India*, 62(3), 246-70

Bumb, B.L. (1972) Regulated marketing in Udaipur district - A case study of Udaipur Mandi, in *Market Towns and Spatial Development*, New Delhi, National Council of Applied Economic Research, 175-78.

Chakravarty, T. (1974) Growth and evolution of the commercial activity in Calcutta, *Proceedings of the Indian Science Congress Association.*

Chandra, R. (1973) Market in a tribal village: Its socio-economic implications among the Bhils, *Vanya-Jati*, 21(2), 52-59.

Chandran, K. (1978) *An Analysis of Marketing Functions in Weekly Markets - The Case Study of Shivaganga*, Unpublished M.Phil. Dissertation, Geography Department, Madurai University.

Chandran, K. (1980) The characteristics of weekly market centre, consumer-trader attendance, and their movement patterns in a micro-region of Tamil Nadu - A case study of Shivaganga taluk, Nagoya, *Proceedings - IGU Congress Working Group on Market Place Exchange Systems.*

Chandran, K. (1983) Consumer and traders attendance and their movement patterns in weekly markets - A case study in Shivaganga taluk, *Proceedings of All India Symposium on Impact of Weekly Markets on Rural Societies*, Geography Department, Madurai University, October 7-10.

Chandran, K. and Swaminathan, E. (1983) Distributional and vocational characteristics of weekly market centres - A case study in Shivaganga taluk weekly markets, *Proceedings of All India Symposium on Impact of Weekly Markets on Rural Societies*, Geography Department, Madurai University, October 7-10.

Chatterjee, A.B. (1965) Hinterland of a symbolic city: Howrah - A case study, *Geographical Review of India*, 27, 55-71.

Chatterjee, A.B. (1969) Nature of commodity flow of a market in the fringe area of Calcutta, *Geographical Review of India*, 31(3), 67-70.

Chaudhary, S. (1975) *Trade and Commercial Organisation in Bengal (1650-1720) with Special Reference to English East india Company*, Calcutta.

Concept (Compiled) (1982) *Who's Who of Geographers in India*, New Delhi, Concept Publishing Company.

Das, M. (1968) Delimitation of the central business district of Calcutta, *Proceedings of the 21st IGU Congress Symposium on Urban Landuse*, Hyderabad.

Das, P.K. (1974) Changing personality of Nandakumar as a market and service centre, *Proceedings - Indian Science Congress Association Session*.

Das, T.K. (1975) Role of market centre in rural economy - A case study in Memari, West Bengal, *The Journal of North-East India Geographical Society*, 7(1-2).

Dayal, P. and Thakur, B. (1976) Commercial ribbons in Patna: spatial growth and functional structure, *The National Geographical Journal of India*, 22, 164-77.

De, J. (1979) Raw material and market as locational factors in the petro-chemical industry, *Geographical Review of India*, 41(3).

De, N.K. (1985) Ecological studies for commercial activities and rural development, *Proceedings of International Conference on Commercial Activities and Rural Development*, Geography Department, Gorakhpur University, December 23-25.

Deb, A.K. (1957) Development of a new port in West Bengal, *Geographical Review of India*, 19(1).

Desai, G.M. (1985) Market channels and growth of fertilizer use in rainfed agriculture: Conceptual considerations and experience in India, in *Agricultural Markets in the Semi-Arid Tropics*, Patancheru, International Crop Research Institute for the Semi-Arid Tropics, 45-52.

Deshpande, C.D. (1941) Market villages and periodic fairs of Bombay-Karnatak, *The Indian Geographical Journal*, 16(4), 327-39.

Dixit, R.S. (1977) On the delimitations of the umland of a metropolis: Kanpur - A case study, *National Geographer*, 12(1), 77-92.

Dixit, R.S. (1979a) *MarketCentres and their Spatial Development in the Umland of Kanpur*, D. Phil. Dissertation, Geography Department, Allahabad University.

Dixit, R.S. (1979b) *Glimpses of the Umland of an Indian Metropolis - The Case of Kanpur*, Lucknow, Mrs. Asha Dixit.

Dixit, R.S. (1980a) Role and rationale of market centres in integrated area development, *Proceedings of Symposium of the Indian Council of Geographers*, January, 19-20.

Dixit, R.S. (1980b) Typology of market centres in the umland of Kanpur based on human number - An empirical study, *Congress Proceedings of National Association of Geographers, India*, January, 34-35.

Dixit, R.S. (1980c) Synchronization of market centres: The case study of the Bundelkhand of the umland of Kanpur, *Congress Proceedings of National Association of Geographers, India*, January, 35.

Dixit, R.S. (1980d) Marketing geography - A bibliographic note, *Uttar Bharat Bhugol Patrika*, 16(1), 70-78.

Dixit, R.S. (1980e) Geographic perspectives in marketing, *Indian Journal of Marketing*, 10(10), 24-27.

Dixit, R.S. (1980f) Hierarchy of market centres in the umland of Kanpur (India), *Newsletter, IGU Working Group on Market Place Exchange Systems*, 9, 12.

Dixit, R.S. (1980g) Role and rationale of market centres in socio-economic development, *Indian Journal of Marketing*, 11(1-2), 21-25.

Dixit, R.S. (1980h) Market synchronization, *The Indian Geographical Journal*, 55(2), 58-61.

Dixit, R.S. (1981a) Classification of market centres based on commodity specialization - The case of the umland of Kanpur metropolis, *Proceedings of Indian Science Congress Association*,

January, 42.

Dixit, R.S. (1981b) Market centres in the umland of Kanpur metropolis - A case study in the application of rank-size relationship, *Congress Proceedings of National Association of Geographers, India*, January.

Dixit, R.S. (1981c) Measuring the transport accessibility of market centres - The case of the umland of Kanpur metropolis, *Congress Proceedings of Indian Science Congress Association*, January, 43.

Dixit, R.S. (1981d) On evolving a systematic network of market centres in the city region of Kanpur metropolis - A step in regional planning, *Proceedings of National Symposium on Regional Planning and Rural Development*, April.

Dixit, R.S. (1981e) Transport accessibility of market centres of Kanpur metropolis, *The Deccan Geographer*, 19(1), 45-52.

Dixit, R.S. (1981f) Market cycles in Bundelkhand, *Congress Proceedings of National Association of Geographers, India*, December.

Dixit, R.S. (1981g) Periodicity: A basis for classification of market centres, *Congress Proceedings of National Association of Geographers, India*, December.

Dixit, R.S. (1981h) Sunday through Saturday: Distribution of market centres in the umland of Kanpur metropolis, *Congress Proceedings of National Association of Geographers, India*, December, 79-80.

Dixit, R.S. (1981i) Market centres in the umland of Kanpur - A case in spatio-temporal changes, *Proceedings of International Conference on Urban and Regional Change in Developing Countries*, December, 1980.

Dixit, R.S. (1981j) Spatio-temporal development of market centres in the umland of Kanpur metropolis during the 20th century, *Congress Proceedings of National Association of Geographers, India*, December, 1979.

Dixit, R.S. (1982a) Market centres in the umland of Kanpur metropolis - Analysis of trade area, *Proceedings of Indian Science Congress Association*, January, 54.

Dixit, R.S. (1982b) Market systems and spatial designs - The case of the Bundelkhand of the umland of Kanpur metropolis, *Proceedings of Indian Science Congress Association*, January, 53-54.

Dixit, R.S. (1982c) Spatial organization of market centres in the umland of a metropolis - A case study, *Indian Journal Landscape Systems*, 5(1-2), 104-120.

Dixit, R.S. (1982d) *Typology of market centres in the umland of Kan-*

pur, Allahabad, G.B.P. Social Science Institute, 1-53.

Dixit, R.S. (1982e) *An exhaustive taxonomical guide for further research work in typology of market centres*, Lucknow, Isabella Thoburn College, 1, 1-24.

Dixit, R.S. (1982f) *Marketing geography - A panoramic view*, Proceedings of Seminar on Geography Teaching and Research, Lucknow, Isabella Thoburn College, October, 1-22.

Dixit, R.S. (1983a) Spatial distribution of market centres in the umland of Kanpur metropolis, *Geographical Review of India*, 45(1), 39-54.

Dixit, R.S, (1983b) Market centres in the umland of Kanpur metropolis - An historical overview prior to the present century, *Newsletter, IGU Working Group on Market Place Exchange Systems*, 13, 4-5.

Dixit, R.S. (1983c) Spatio-temporal development of market centres in the umland of Kanpur metropolis during the present century, *Newsletter, IGU Working Group on Market Place Exchange Systems*, 13, 5.

Dixit, R.S. (1983d) Sunday through Saturday, *The Indian Geographical Journal*, 58(2), 196-97.

Dixit, R.S. (1983e) Market systems and spatial designs, *Vikas Sheel Bhugol Patrika*, 2(2), 115-18.

Dixit, R.S. (1983f) *Marketing geography - A view*, Lucknow, Isabella Thoburn College, 2, 1-22.

Dixit, R.S. (1984a) Distribution of market centres, *Indian Journal of Marketing Geography*, 2(1), 14-20.

Dixit, R.S. (1984b) Market centres and their spatial development in the umland of Kanpur, *Vikas Sheel Bhugol Patrika*, 3(2), 72-74.

Dixit, R.S. (1984c) Market cycles, *Indian Journal of Marketing Geography*, 2(2), 102-105.

Dixit, R.S. (1984d) Transport connectivity of market centres in the umland of Kanpur, *The Indian Geographical Journal*, 59(2), 181-86.

Dixit, R.S. (1984e) Classification of market centres in the umland of Kanpur, *Landscape Systems and Ecological Studies*, 7(2), 57-62.

Dixit, R.S. (1984f) Role of small and medium towns in the context of regional development, *Proceedings of World Congress on Human Settlements in Developing Countries*, December, 20.

Dixit, R.S. (1984g) *Market Centres and their Spatial Development in the Umland of Kanpur*, Allahabad, Kitab Mahal.

Dixit, R.S. (1984h) *Spatial Organisation of Market Centres in Hamirpur District, U.P. (India)*, Research Project Report, New Delhi, Indian Council of Social Science Research.

Dixit, R.S. (1985a) Typology of market centres based on marketing hours, *Proceedings of Indian Science Congress Association*, January, 56.

Dixit, R.S. (1985b) Traders' movement and travel patterns - A case study of Hamirpur district, U.P. (India), *Transaction - Indian Council of Geographers*, 15, 11-14.

Dixit, R.S. (1985c) Spatial organization of market centres in the umland of a metropolis, Kanpur - A case study, *Proceddings of IGU International Workshop on Agricultural Markets in the Semi-Arid Tropics*, October, 155.

Dixit, R.S. (1985d) Typology of market centres based on human number, in S.C.Mukhopadhyaya (ed.) *Geographical Mosaic*, Calcutta Modern Book Agency, 722-33.

Dixit, R.S. (1985e) Market centres of a backward economy - Hamirpur district, U.P. (India) - Chronological perspective, *The Deccan Geographer*, 23(3), 132-45.

Dixit, R.S. (1985f) Typology of market centres based on marketing hours – The case of the District Hamirpur, U.P. (India), *Vikas Sheet Bhugol Patrika*, 4(1-2), 42-45.

Dixit, R.S. (1985g) Spatial organization of market centres in Hamirpur district, U.P. India, in E. Gormsen (ed.) *Market Place Research*, Mainz, Geographisches Institut Der Johannes-Gutenberg Universitat, 107-08.

Dixit, R.S. (1985h) Market centres of a backward economy - Hamirpur district, U.P. (India), *Proceedings of IGU Conference on Study Group Geography of Commercial Activities*, December, 21.

Dixit, R.S. (1986a) Market centres of a backward economy - Hamirpur district, U.P. India - Perspectives on distribution, *Proceedings of Indian Science Congress Association*, January, 39-40.

Dixit, R.S. (1986b) Market centres of a backward economy - Hamirpur district, U.P. India - Perspectives on trade area, *Transactions - Indian Council of Geographers*, 16, 29-41.

Dixit, R.S. (1986c) Market cycles in Hamirpur district, U.P. (India), *Geographical Review of India*, 48(2), 34-40.

Dixit, R.S. (1986d) Market centres of a backward economy - Hamirpur district, U.P. India - Perspectives on market cycles, *Landscape Systems and Ecological Studies*, 9(1), 121-26.

Dixit, R.S. (1986e) Role of market centres in regional development and their spatial planning in the metropolitan region of Kanpur, in L.R. Singh (ed.) *Regional Planning and Rural Development*, Allahabad,

Thinkers' Library, 183-210.

Dixit, R.S. (1986f) Geography of commercial activities - Furtherance of marketing geography, *The Indian National Geographer*, 1(1-2), 98-108.

Dixit, R.S. (1986g) Role of small and medium towns in the context of regional development, in K.P. Bhattacharya (ed.) *Human Settlement in Developing Countries*, Calcutta, Habitat Centre. 213-218.

Dixit, R.S. (1987a) Market centres of Hamirpur district U.P. (India), *Proceedings of Indian Science Congress Association*, January, 70-71.

Dixit, R.S. (1987b) Development strategy for a small town - The case of Mahoba, U.P. (India), *Proceedings of Third International Congress on Human Settlements in Developing Countries*, January, 13.

Dixit. R.S. (1987c) Slums of Uttar Pradesh: The case of the two KAVAL towns, *Proceedings of National Seminar on Environment and Ecology*, February, 213.

Dixit, R.S. (1987d) Distribution of market centres in a backward economy - Hamirpur district, U.P. (India), *The National Geographical Journal of India*, 33(1), 80-88.

Dixit, R.S. (1987e) Glimpses of the umland of a metropolis - The case of Kanpur, in C.S. Yadav (ed.) *Perspectives in Urban Geography, Vol. IX, Rural Urban Fringe*, New Delhi, Concept Publishing Company.

Dixit, R.S. (1988a) Market centres of a backward economy - Perspectives on centrality and hierarchy, in V.K. Srivastava (ed.) *Commercial Activities and Rural Development in South Asia*, New Delhi, Concept Publishing Company, 159-174.

Dixit, R.S. (1988b) *Marketing Geography: The Indian Scenario - Inventory and Prospects*, Post-Doctoral Research Project Report, New Delhi, Indian Council of Social Science Research.

Dixit, R.S. (1989) *Periodic Marketing in an Urban Environment - Mahoba: A Case Study in Geography of Marketing and Commercial Activities*, Post-Doctoral Research Project Report, New Delhi, University Grants Commission.

Dixit, R.S. and Verma, D.N. (1980) Marketing geography - A bibliographic note, *Uttar Bharat Bhugol Patrika*, 16(1), 70-78.

Dixit, R.S. and Verma, D.N. (1988) An inventory of bibliographies on geography of marketing and commerical activities in India, *Geographical Rev. of India*, 50, 1, March, 84-87.

Doshi, A. (1983) Complex dimensions of rural marketing, *Commerce*,

147(3763), July 16, 92-93.

Dube, R.S. (1985) A rational approach to the marketing of foodgrains in M.P., *Proceedings of International Conference: Commercial Activities and Rural Development*, Department of Geography, Gorakhpur University, December 23-25.

Duggal, S.L. and Mullick, H.S. (1974) A classification of agricultural markets in Haryana, *Geographical Observer*, 10, 73-78.

Dutta, A.K. (1966a) Daily shopping in Calcutta, *Town Planning Review*, 37, 207-16.

Dutta, A.K. (1966b) Daily shopping in Howrah city, *The National Geographical Journal of India*, 12(3), 163-77.

Dutta, A.K. (1972) Daily influence area of Calcutta, *Journal of Tropical Geography*, 25, 32-39.

Dutta, A.K. and Harrity, P.B. (1972) Drawing power of the daily shopping centres in Calcutta and its correlates, *Geographical Review of India*, 34(3), 249-61.

Dwivedi, S. (1982) Patterns of external trade in a colonial setting – A case study of north-eastern Plateau (1884-1947), *The National Geographical Journal of India*, 28(3-4), 127-33.

Fox, R.G. (1967) Family, caste and commerce in a north Indian market town, *Economic Development and Regional Change*, 15, 297-314.

Fox, R.G. (1979) Influence of periodic markets on the occupational structure of rural settlements, *The Deccan Geographer*, 17(1), 555-558.

Garg, P.K. (1972a) Reorientation of policy for the development of market towns, in *Market Towns and Spatal Development*, New Delhi, National Council of Applied Economic Research, 125-26.

Garg, P.K. (1972b) Small townships: A perspective for development, in *Market Towns and Spatial Development*, New Delhi, National Council of Applied Economic Research, 113-18.

Gedam, D.A. (1974) A geographical analysis of fairs at Salbardi, *Indian Geographical Journal*, 49(1), 17-24.

Gedam, D.A. (1978) *The Marketing System and Network in the Wardha Valley*, Unpublished Ph. D. Dissertation, Geography Department, Nagpur University.

Gedam, D.A. (1980) Hierarchy of periodic market centres in the Wardha valley of Maharashtra, *Landscape Systems and Ecological Studies*, 3(1-2).

Gedam, D.A. (1981) The origin conditions of periodic market places in the Wardha valley of Maharashtra, *The Deccan Geographer*, 19(2-

3), 79-89.

Gedam, D.A. (1983) Typology of service area of periodic marketing system and network, *Transactions - Institute of Indian Geographers*, 5(1).

Gedam, D.A. (1984) The transportation system of periodic market centres in the Wardha valley of Maharashtra, *The Indian Journal of Marketing Geography*, 2(1-2), 28-33.

Gedam, D.A. (1985a) Spatio-temporal spacing of periodic markets in the Wardha valley of Maharashtra, in *Regional Geography of the World*, Patna, Geographical Research Centre.

Gedam, D.A. (1985b) Sellers' travel behaviour and periodic market cycles in the Wardha valley, *Proceedings of International Conference on Commercial Activities and Rural Development*, Geography Department, Gorakhpur University, December, 23-25.

Geetha, T. (1977) *A Spatial Analysis of Periodic Markets in Krishnagiri Taluk*, M. Phil. Dissertation, Faculty of Science, Madras University.

Geetha, T. (1978) The size of communities and area served by periodic markets in Krishnagiri taluk, Tamil Nadu, India, *Oriental Geographer*, 12(1-2).

Ghosal, K. (1972) Market places and market areas, *National Geographer*, 7, 85-94.

Gosh, M. and Mitra, G. (1982) Market centre - An important type of settlement in north Bengal, *Geographical Review of India*, 44(1), 19-29.

Gopi, K.N. and Dunkerley, J. (1985) Fuelwood markets in Hyderabad, in *Agricultural Markets in the Semi-Arid Tropics*, Patancheru, International Crop Research Institute for the Semi-Arid Tropics, 109-120.

Gormsen, E. (1985) *Market Place Research*, Mainz, Geographisches Institut der Johannes - Gutenberg Universitat.

Gupta, N.L. and Hiren, S.L. (1972) Surplus/deficit area of food production in Rajasthan in 1961-66, *The Indian Geographical Journal*, 47(3-4).

Gupta, S.K. (1967) The landscape of milk supply at Baraut, *The Geographical Observer*, 3.

Gupta, V.K. (1972) The system of cities and towns in relation to economic development in India, in *Market Towns and Spatial Development*, New Delhi, National Council of Applied Economic Research, 104-12.

Hall, K. (1977) Price marketing and market hierarchy in early medieval south India, *Indian Economic and Social Historical Review*, 14(2), 223-30.

Harriss, B. (1975) Poverty, caste, rurality of transactions: A speculative explanation for periodic marketing in northern Tamil Nadu, *Proceedings – Second Indo-British Seminar*, Cambridge.

Harriss, B. (1976) Social specificity in rural weekly market - The case of northern Tamil Nadu, India, *IGU Working Group on Market Distribution System*, 23rd International Geography Congress, Moscow.

Harriss, B. (1979) State intervention of dryland foodgrains markets and price inequality in Andhra Pradesh and Karnatak States, *Proceedings of the Third Indo-British Geography Seminar*, Madras, Tripati and Mysore, December, 8-17.

Harriss, B. (1980a) Regulated foodgrains markets : A critique, *Social Scientist, India*, 9(2), 22-31.

Harriss, B. (1980b) Inaction, interaction, and action - Regulated agricultural markets in Tamil Nadu, *Social Scientist, India*, 9(4), 96-137.

Harriss, B. (1981a) *Transitional Trade and Rural Development*, New Delhi, Vikas Publishing House.

Harriss, B. (1981b) The distribution of agricultural mercantile power in Tamil Nadu, in *Transactions: Centre for Regional Ecological and Science Studies in Development Alternatives*, 1, 19-28.

Harriss, B. (1983a) Relations of production and exchange and poverty in rain-fed agricultural regions, *Economic and Political Weekly*, 18, 24/9/83, A82-A92.

Harriss, B. (1983b) Implementation of food distribution policies - A case study in south India, *Food Policy*, 121-30.

Harriss, B. (1984a) *State and Market*, New Delhi, Concept Publishing Company.

Harriss, B. (1984b) *Exchange Relations and Poverty in Dryland Agriculture*, New Delhi, Concept Publishing Company.

Harriss, B. (1985) Agricultural markets and inter-sectoral resource transfers: Cases from the Semi-Arid Tropics of South-East India, in *Agricultural Markets in the Semi-Arid Tropics*, Patancheru, International Crop Research Institute for the Semi-Arid Tropics, 279-304.

Hashim, S.R. (1972) Town size and functions, in *Market Towns and Spatial Development*, New Delhi, National Council of Applied

Economic Research, 127-135.

Hirt, H.F. (1975) The oriental bazaar - A case study for India, *The Indian Geographical Journal*, 50(1), 13-24.

Hugar, S.I. (1984) *Spatial Analysis of Market Systems in Dharwad District*, Unpublished Ph. D. Dissertation, Geography Department, Karnatak University.

Hugar, S.I. (1985) Periodic Non-periodic marketing and rural development in Dharwad district, *Proceedings of International Conference on Commercial Activities and Rural Development*, Geography Department, Gorakhpur University, December, 23-25.

Hussain, S.A. (1937) *Agricultural Marketing in Northern India*, London, George Allan and Unwin.

ICRISAT (1985) *Agricultural Markets in the Semi-Arid Tropics*, Patancheru, International Crop Research Institute for the Semi-Arid Tropics.

ICSSR (1972) *A Survey of Research in Geography*, Bombay, Popular Prakashan (for Indian Council of Social Science Research, New Delhi).

ICSSR (1979) *A Survey of Research in Geography (1969-72)*, New Delhi, Allied Publishers (P) Ltd. (for the Indian Council of Social Science Research, New Delhi).

ICSSR (1975-1982) *ICSSR Journal of Abstracts and Reviews : Geography* - 8 volumes: 1975 - 1982, New Delhi, Concept Publishing Company.

ICSSR (1984) *A Survey of Research in Geography (1972-75)*, New Delhi, Concept Publishing Company (for the Indian Council of Social Science Research, New Delhi).

IGU (1972-1985) *Newsletters of the International Geographical Union Working Group on Market Place Exchange Systems*, Nos. 1 to 15, International Geographical Union for Working Group on Market Place Exchange Systems.

IGU (1986-1988) *Newsletters of the International Geographical Union Study Group: Geography of Commercial Activities*, Nos. 1 to 5, International Geographical Union Study Group Commission: Geography of Commercial Activities.

INDIA (Undated) *Survey Report on Rural Market Development Programme*, New Delhi.

INDIA (1979) *The Third Indo-British Geography Seminar, Abstracts*, Madras, Tirupati, Mysore, December 8-17.

INDIA (1980) *Workshop on Rural Market Centre Development*

Programme - Asian Regional Evaluation, Abstracts, Bangalore.

INDIA (1982a) *National Workshop on Regulation and Management of Agricultural Produce Markets, Abstracts*, Directorate of Marketing and Inspection, Ranchi - April 1981, Faridabad, New Delhi, Pune - May 1982.

INDIA (1982b) *International Conference on Improving Geographical Accessibility of Rural Services, Abstracts*, July 1982, Indian Institute of Management, Bangalore.

INDIA (1983a) *Symposium on Impact of Weekly Markets on Rural Societies, Abstracts*, Madurai University, October 7-10.

INDIA (1983b) *Agricultural Markets in Semi-Arid Tropics, Abstracts*, International Workshop on Agricultural Markets in Semi-Arid Tropics, Hyderabad, ICRISAT, October-November, 1983.

INDIA (1984) *National Workshop on Regulation and Management of Agricultural Produce Markets, Abstracts*, Jaipur, February.

INDIA (1985a) *Fourth National Workshop on Agricultural Markets, Abstracts*, Lucknow.

INDIA (1985b) *International Conference: Commercial Activities and Rural Development, Abstracts*, Gorakhpur University, December 23-25.

Ishihara, H. (1961) Markets in West Bengal - An Analysis of District Census Handbook, *The Journal of the Faculty of Literature*, 80.

Ishihara, H. (1978) Markets in Howrah District, West Bengal, in *Professor Fujioka's commemoration Historico-Geographical Studies and Urban Studies*, Tokyo, Taimeido Publications.

Ishihara, H. (1979) Markets in Hooghly District, West Bengal, *The Journal of the Faculty of Literature*, The Thirtieth Anniversary Volume.

Ishihara, H. (1983a) Traditional markets and areal demand density in India, *The Journal of the Faculty of Literature*, Volume 83.

Ishihara, H. (1983b) Distribution of Markets in India and Bangladesh, *The Journal of the Faculty of Literature*, Volume 86.

Ishihara, H. (1985a) *General Survey of Traditional Markets in Tamil Nadu, South India, in Professor J. Hosai Commemoration chiiki o mequru.*

Ishihara, H. (1985b) *Rural Markets in South India*, School of Letters, August.

Ishihara, H. (1988) *Markets and Marketing in South India*, Nagoya, School of Letters, University of Nagoya.

Jain, C.K. and Sharma, S.K. (1986) Agricultural marketing in M.P.,

Geographical Review of India, 48(3), 59-69.

Jain, N.G. (1975) Retail shopping centres of Nagpur West - Landuse and planning, *The Deccan Geographer*, 13(1-2), 145-56.

Jamkar, A.G. (1984) Spatial distribution of spatio-temporal analysis of periodic market places in Dhule district, *The Deccan Geographer*, 22(3), 532-37.

Jamkar, A.G. (1985) Origin and evolution of periodic market place in Dhule district, *Proceedings of International Conference on Commercial Activities and Rural Development*, Geography Department, Gorakhpur University, December 23-25.

Jamuna, K., Swaminathan, E. and Nallasivam, S. (1983) An understanding towards the locational characteristics, functional organization and trade area of Allinagram weekly market, Madurai district, *Proceedings of All India Symposium on Impact of Weekly Markets on Rural Societies*, Geography Department, Madurai University, October 7-10.

Jana, M.M. (1978) Hierarchy of market centres in lower Silabati Basin, *Geographical Review of India*, 40(2), 164-74.

Jana, M.M. (1986) Retail centres in lower Silabati Basin, *Geographical Review of India*, 48(1), 64-72.

Janaki, V.K. (1962) Tributary area of Baroda, *Journal of M.S. University of Baroda*, 11, 81-99.

Jayashankar, D.C. (1976) Delineation of hinterland of ports – Methods and techniques - with a case study of Madras, Vishakhapatnam, and Cochin, in V.L.S.P. Rao and others (ed.) *Readings in Planning and Development*, Silver Jubilee Volume, Indian Geographical Society, 174-87.

Jayashankar, D.C. (1979) Marketing as a catalyst for regional development – A case study of Karnataka, *Proceedings of the Third Indo-British Geography Seminar*, Madras, Tirupati, Mysore, December 8-17.

Jayashankar, D.C. (1984) Marketing geography, in *A Survey of Research in Geography (1972-75)*, New Delhi, Indian Council of Social Science Research.

Jayaswal, S.N.P. (1963) Bindki - A case study in the evolution of a trade centre, *The National Geographical Journal of India*, 9(3-4), 187-200.

Jodha, N.S. (1985) Market forces and erosion of common property resources, in *Agricultural Markets in the Semi-Arid Tropics*, Patancheru, International Crop Research Institute for the Semi-Arid

Tropics, 263-78.

Johnson, E.A.J. (1972) The integration of agrarian, commercial and industrial activities in functional economic areas, in *Market Towns and Spatial Developments*, New Delhi, National Council of Applied Economic Research, 57-76.

Jogaiah, T. (1983) The usefulness of weekly markets, *Kurukshetra*, 31(8), January 16, 11-13.

Joseph, S.E. (1972) Industrial dispersal in India, in *Market Towns and Spatial Development* New Delhi, National Council of Applied Economic Research, 121-24.

Joshi, S. (1987) The spatial pattern of drug retailing in Pune, *The National Geographical Journal of India*, 33(1), 35-48.

Joshi, V.K. (1971) *Regular Markets in Gujarat*, Sardar Patel University.

Jothimai, P. and Swaminathan, E. (1983) An analysis of functional morphology and the movement of traders, farmers and buyers - A case study on Udumalpet weekly market, *Proceedings of All India Symposium on Impact of weekly markets on Rural Societies*, Geography Department, Madurai University, October 7-10.

Kahlon, S.S. and Kehal, H.S. (1972) Market towns in Punjab and their impact on rural development, in *Market Towns and Spatial Development*, New Delhi, National Council of Applied Economic Research, 196-200.

Kala, S.C. (1976) Model markets in U.P. towns, *Times of India*, July 2, 4.

Kara, P.K. (1985) Delimitation of the hinterland overlap of Paradip port, *The Journal of North-East India Geographical Society*, 17 (1-2).

Karwe, I. and Acharya, H. (1970) *The Role of Weekly Markets – in the Tribal, Rural, and Urban Setting*, ICSSR Report,Poona, Deccan College.

Karwe, K.R. (1951) *Agricultural Marketing in India*, 2 Vols., Bombay, Cooperative Book Depot.

Katiyar, R.C. (1985) Spatio-temporal and functional pattern of rural markets - A case study of Farrukhabad district, U.P., *Transactions: Indian Council of Geographers*, 15, 52-54.

Katiyar, R.C. and Singh, K. (1981) Market centres of Hamirpur tehsil - A geographical analysis, *Transactions: Indian Council of Geographers*, 9.

Kayastha, S.L. (1963) Kandla - A case study in port development, *The*

National Geographical Journal of India, 9(1).

Khan, W. (1967) *Market Settlements in Hyderabad Metropolitan Region*, Technical Bulletin No. 5, Hyderabad, Metropolitan Research Project.

Khan, W. (1972) Market centres in Chevella Taluk - A descriptive analysis, in *Market Towns and Spatial Development*, New Delhi, National Council of Applied Economic Research, 192-95.

Khandwe, M.A. (1982) Distribution pattern and classification of market centres in the Amravati district, *The Deccan Geographer*, 20(2), 257-62.

Krishan, G. (1963) Spatial analysis and vegetable supply to a planned city - Chandigarh, *The National Geographical Journal of India*, 16, 1-15.

Krishan, G. and Agarwal, S.K. (1973) Commercial pattern of a planned city - Chandigarh, *The National Geographical Journal of India*, 19.

Krishan, G. (1983) Functional classification of weekly markets in south India, *Proceedings of All India Symposium on the Impact of Weekly Markets on Rural Societies*, Geography Department, Madurai University, October 7-10.

Krishnamorthy, B. (1983) A study on weekly cattle market centre, Madurai Thursday Cattle Market - A case study, *Proceedings of All India Symposium on the Impact of Weekly Markets on Rural Societies*, Geography Department, Madurai University, October 7-10.

Krishnan, V. (1932) Fairs and trade centres of Madurai and Ramnad districts, *Journal of Madras Geographical Association*, 7(3), 237-49.

Krishanan, V. (1933) Fairs, festivals and shandies in Trichy district, *Journal of Madras Geographical Association*, 8(3).

Krishnan, V. (1940) Trade centres in Tinnevelly district, *Journal of Madras Geographical Association*, 15(2-3), 272-76.

Kulkarni, K.M. (1980) Shopping centres in Nasik city, *Geographical Reviews of India*, 42(3).

Kulkarni, G.S. (1962) Service area of market centre in the Transitional Mysore State - Yamakanmardi - A case study, *Bombay Geographical Magazine*, 10(1), 86-96.

Kulkarni, G.S. (1972) Market centres in western India, in W.P. Adams and Hellener, F.M. (eds.) *International Geography*, 2(22) Toronto, IGU Congress, 1295-97.

Kulkarni, K.R. (1951) *Agricultural Marketing in India*, 2 volumes, Bombay, Co-operative Book Depot.

Kumar, A. and Sharma, N. (1977) Rural centres of services - A case study of Sundega, *Geographical Review of India*, 39(1), 19-29.

Kumar, S. (1980a) Spatial dimensions in retailing, in R.B. Mandal and V.N.P. Sinha (eds.) *Recent Trends and Concepts in Geography*, Vol. 2, New Delhi, Concept Publishing Company, 171-78.

Kumar, S. (1980b) The concept of consumer behaviour, in R.B. Mandal and V.N.P. Sinha (eds.) *Recent Trends and Concepts in Geography*, Vol. 2, New Delhi, Concept Publishing Company, 179-92.

Kumaran, T.V. (1983) Markets cooperatives and marketing in Kolli Hills, *Proceedings of All India Symposium on the Impact of Weekly Markets on Rural Societies*, Geography Department, Madurai University, October 7-10.

Kumavat, B.L. (1973) *Market Towns of the Central Aravali*, Unpublished Ph. D. Dissertation, Geography Department, Udaipur University.

Kumbhar, A.P. and Deshmukh, P.W. (1984a) Periodic markets and regional links in Sangli district, *The Deccan Geographer*, 22(3), 538-48.

Kumbhar, A.P. and Deshmukh, P.W. (1984b) Specialized market centres of Sangli district (Maharashtra): Some observations, *The Indian Journal of Marketing Geography*, 2(1-2), 98-101.

Lahiri, T.B. (1972) Development of townships - Policies and problems, in *Market towns and Spatial Development*, New Delhi, National Council of Applied Economic Research, 136-38.

Lal, H. and Yadav, H.R. (1985) Development of commercial activities in Gorakhpur citty, *Proceedings of International Conference on Commercial Activities in Rural Development*, Geography Department, Gorakhpur University, December 23-25.

Lal, R.S. (1974) Revelganj - A study in changing pattern of a market town, *Indian Geographical Studies*, 3, 21-27.

Lal, V.N. (1985) Commercial activities in a small town: A case study of Bachharawan town in U.P., *Proceedings of International Conference on Commercial Activities in Rural Development*, Geography Department, Gorakhpur University, December 23-25.

Lal, V.N. and Gupta, V.P. (1983) Baberu - A study in marketing Geography, *The Indian Journal of Marketing Geography*, 1(1-2).

Leon, S. (1979) *The North Indian Peasant Goes to Market*, Delhi, Motilal Banarsidas.

Mahalanobis, J.N. (1972) Development of townships - Policies and problems, in *Market Towns and Spatial Development*, New Delhi, National Council of Applied Economic Research, 103.

Mahalay, K.L. (1973) The rise and fall in the commercial significance of the Deccan caves, *The Deccan Geographer*, 2(1-2).

Mahato, S.N. (1974) Organization of trade in rural area of Ranchi district, *Bulletin of the Cultural Research Institute*, 10(1-2), 86-91.

Maidamwar, G.T. (1979a) Morphological features of livestock market places - A regional case study of Yavatmal district, *The Deccan Geographer*, 17(2), 605-14.

Maidamwar, G.T. (1979b) *Livestock Marketing Network and System in Yavatmal District*, Unpublished Ph. D. Dissertation, Geography Department, Nagpur University.

Maikap, A.K. (1972) Role of market centres in Indian economic development with special reference to West Bengal,in *Market Towns and Spatial Development*, New Delhi, National Council of Applied Economic Research, 183-86.

Malshe, P.T. (1979) Influence of periodic markets on the occupational structure of rural settlements, *The Deccan Geographer*, 17(1).

Mandal, H. (1985) Growth of market centres in Nagpur city, *Geographical Review of India*, 47(1), 13-18.

Mani, K.C. *et al.* (1981) Factors associated with participants and non-participants attitude towards regulated markets, *Indian Journal of Extension Education*, 17(3-4), 31-43.

Master, M.A. (1953) Problems facing Indian Shipping, *Andhra Chamber of Commerce, Silver Jubilee Volume I*.

Mathai, P.M. (1972) Growth centres, in *Market Towns and Spatial Development*, New Delhi, National Council of Applied Economic Research, 85-88.

Mathur, G. (1972) Innovations in building for speedier development of towns of economical cost, in *Market Towns and Spatial Development*, New Delhi, National Council of Applied Economic Research, 96-98.

Mathur, R.S. (1982) Consumer behaviour in markets of Jaipur's walled city, *Indian Geographical Studies*, 19, 28-41.

Mathur, V.S. (1941) Agricultural marketing in western United Provinces, *Indian Geographical Journal*, 16(1), 28-41.

Mehtra, I. (1980) A bi-weekly market in a north Indian village, *Eastern Anthropologist*, 33(2), 154-58.

Menon, K.P.A. (1985) Market channels and farmers' access to improved seed for rain-fed agriculture, in *Agricultural Markets in the Semi-Arid tropics*, Patancheru, International Crop Research Institute for the Semi-Arid Tropics, 15-20.

Metton, A. (ed.) (1986-88) *Newsletters IGU Study Group: Geography of Commercial Activities*, 1-5.

Miltendorf, H.J. (1982) Rural market centre - Potential development centre for small farmer development, *Indian Journal of Public Administration*, 28(1), 101-19.

Mitra, A. (1953) *Fairs and Festivals in Western Bengal*, Alipore, Government Press.

Mohanty, P. (1972) Tribal market in Parlekhabadi agency, *Adivasi*, 12.

Mohanty, S.K. (1980) *Hierarchy of Market Centres in Lower Mahanadi-Brahmani Basin*, Unpublished Ph.D. Dissertation, Geography Department, Utkal University.

Mohanty, S.K. and Singh, D.K. (1980) Domestic market potential of the lower Mahanadi-Brahmani Basin in Orissa, *Eastern Geographical Research Bulletin*, 13.

Moharana, B.B. (1977) A weekly tribal market in Orissa, *Journal of Social Research*, 20(2), 41-53.

Mukherjee, A.B. (1955) Economic trends in the markets of central Birbhum, *The Geographical Review of India*, 17(2).

Mukherjee, A.B. (1957) The bi-weekly market at Modinagar, *Indian Geographer*, 2(2), 271-93.

Mukherjee, M. (1970) Trade towns of Bihar, *The Geographical Knowledge*, 3(1-2), 1-14.

Mukherjee, S.P. (1968) Commercial activity and market hierarchy in a part of eastern Himalaya, Darjeeling, *The National Geographical Journal of India*, 14(2-3), 186-199.

Murty, K.N. and Oppen, M. von (1985) Nutrients distribution and consumer preferences in India: Some policy implications, in *Agricultural Markets in the Semi-Arid Tropics*, Patancheru, International Crop Research Institute for the Semi-Arid Tropics, 179-200.

Murugesan, N. and Swaminathan, E. (1983) Functional morphology and the movement of traders and consumers - A case study of Pudansandai weekly market, Nammakkal taluk, *Proceedings of All India Symposium on Impact of Weekly Markets on Rural Societies*, Geography Department, Madurai University, October 7-10.

Muthiah, C. (1972) Role of regulated markets in the development process - A case study for Tamil Nadu, in *Market Towns and Spatial Development*, New Delhi, National Council of Applied

Economic Research, 155-59.

Nadkarni, M.V. (1985) The role of agricultural markets and market policy - Not conducive to rural welfare, in *Agricultural Markets in the Semi-Arid Tropics*, Patancheru, International Crop Research Institute for the Semi-Arid Tropics, 243-50.

Nageswari, S. and Gopalakrishanan, K.S. (1983) An analysis of spatial distribution of weekly markets in Tamil Nadu State, *Proceedings of All India Symposium on the Impact of Weekly Markets on Rural Societies*, Geography Department, Madurai University, October 7-10.

Narayan, B.S. (1981) Towards evolution of regulated market system in Kerala, *Yojana*, 25(21) November 16, 27-28.

Nath, T. and Kushwaha, R.K. (1985) The role of market centres in rural development - A case study of Rampur Karkhana block, *Proceedings of International Conference on Commercial Activities and Rural Development*, Geography Department, Gorakhpur University, December 23-25.

Nath, V. (1983) *Marketing and Social Structure in North Avadh Plain*, Unpublished Ph.D. Dissertation, Geography Department, Gorakhpur University.

Nath, V. and Jain, A.K. (1981) Fairs in Avadh Plain, *Uttar Bharat Bhugol Patrika*, 17(2).

Nath, V. and Nath, T. (1985) An analytical survey of consumer trader behaviour in Avadh Plain, *Proceedings of International Conference on Commercial Activities and Rural Development*, Geography Department, Gorakhpur University, December 23-25.

Nayak, H.P. (1982) Krishi Bazar Kendra, U.P., *Vikas Sheel Bhugol Patrika*, 1(1).

NCAER (1965a) *Market Towns and Spatial Development in India*, New Delhi, National Council of Applied Economic Research.

NCAER (1965b) *Techno-Economic Survey of Uttar Pradesh*, New Delhi, National Council of Applied Economic Research.

NCAER (1971) *Seminar on Market Towns and Spatial Development*, NCAER for Department of Works, Housing and Urban Development, Government of India, New Delhi, April.

NCAER (1972a) Background note on development of market towns, in *Market Towns and Spatial Development*, New Delhi, National Council of Applied Economic Research, 33-56.

NCAER (1972b) Planning and development of towns - New and existing criteria for selection, in *Market Towns and Spatial Develop-*

ment, New Delhi, National Council of Applied Economic Research, 27-29.

NCAER (1972c) The role of market centres in the development process, in *Market Towns and Spatial Development*, New Delhi, National Council of Applied Economic Research, 17-21..

NCAER (1972d) Towns as levers of industrial spread and role of industrial estates, in *Market Towns and Spatial Development*, New Delhi, National Council of Applied Economic Research, 22-26.

NCAER (1972e) *Market Towns and Spatial Development*, New Delhi, National Council of Applied Economic Research.

Neale, W. *et al.* (1965) Kurali market - A report on the economic geography of marketing in northern Punjab, *Economic Development and Cultural Change*, 13, 129-68.

Nolakha, R.L. (1976) *Marketing of Handicraft in Rajasthan*, Unpublished Ph. D. Dissertation, Rajasthan University.

Pal, M.K. (1978) *Crafts and Craftsmen in Traditional India*, New Delhi, Kanak Publications.

Pandyan, S.R. (1937) Nagapatnam - A sea-port town, *Journal of Madras Geographical Association*, 11(4).

Pant, D. (1930) *The Commercial Policy of Moghuls*, Bombay.

Parvathi, C. (1975a) Market system and market centre locations - Pollachi tract, *Proceedings of South-East Asian Regional Conference in Applied Geography*, Singapore.

Parvathi, C. (1975b) The structure of an Indian market town - Pollachi - A case study, *Proceedings of Indo-British Geographical Seminar on Rural Urban Interaction*, Cambridge.

Parvathi, C. (1976) The structure of market town region - Pollacchi - A case study, *The Indian Geographical Society, Golden Jubilee Vol.* 76-91.

Parvathi, C. (1978) *Market Centres and Spatial Development - A Case Study of Coimbatore-Nilgiri Region*, Unpublished Ph. D. Dissertation, Geography Department, Mysore University.

Prakash, Rao, V.L.S. (1961) *Bhongiri - A case study in Market Town*, Census of India Monograph 12, New Delhi, Registrar General, Ministry of Health.

Patel. A.M. (1963) The rural markets of Rajshahi district, *Oriental Geographer*, 7.

Patil, B. (1975) Development of regulated markets in Bijapur district, *March of Karnataka*, 11(4), 13-14.

Patil, S.P. and Pawat, J.R. (1980) *A Study of Marketing of Fruits in*

Mahatona Phule Market Bombay, Department of Agricultural Economics, Mahatona Phule Krishi.

Pattanaik, N. (1953) Weekly market at Barpali, *The Geographical Review of India*, 15(1), 19-31.

Paul, M.S. (1933) The commercial geography of Udayapalayam taluk, *The Indian Geographical Journal*, 8(3).

Ponniah, J.S. (1940) Cotton and cotton markets in Tinnevelly district, *Journal of Madras Geographical Association*, 15(3).

Prasad, A. (1978) Our regulated markets, *Andhra Pradesh*, 22(8), 19-21.

Prasad, I. (1975) On delineating of market region, *Geographical Outlook*, 11, 127-40.

Punja, H.G. (1938) Coffee trade in Mangalore, *Journal of Madras Geographical Association*, 13(3).

Raju, V.T. and Bhatt, B.D. (1985) Efficiency in pricing and operation of markets for semi-arid tropical crops in India - A case of groundnut in Gujarat, in *Agricultural Markets in Semi-Arid Tropics*, Patancheru, International Crop Research Institute for the Semi-Arid Tropics, 210.

Raju, V.T. and Oppen von, M. (1980) *Market Channels for Selected Crops in Semi-Arid Tropical India*, Patancheru, International Crop Research Institute for the Semi-Arid Tropics.

Raju, V.T. and Oppen von, M. (1982) *Marketing Efficiency for Selected Crops in Semi-Arid Tropical India*, Patancheru, International Crop Research Insitute for the Semi-Arid Tropics.

Ram, U. (1982) *Priodic Markets and Rural Development in the Lower Ganga-Ghaghara Doab*, Unpublished Ph.D. Dissertation, Geography Department, Gorakhpur University.

Ram, U. and Srivastava, V.K. (1982) Nature and demarcation of market area regions of lower Ganga-Ghaghara Doab, *Uttar Bharat Bhugol Patrika*, 18(2), 97-107.

Ramachandran, H. (1982) *Behaviour in Space - Rural Marketing in Under Developed Economy*, New Delhi, Concept Publishing Company.

Ramakrishna, K.C. (1931-32) Markets for Malabar produce, *Journal of Madras Geographical Association*, 6(3-4).

Ramakrishna, K.C. (1939) Milk supply in Madras, *The Indian Geographical Journal*, 14(4).

Ramakrishnan, N. (1969) Shandy in Tamil Nadu, *Social Welfare*, 16(3).

Ramamurthy, K. (1938) Trade of Madras port, *Journal of Madras Geographical Association*, 13(4).

Ramanandham, V.V. and Krishnamurthi, R. (1955) Ports of Andhra, *The Indian Geographical Journal*, 20(4).

Ramaswamy, G. and Shivamurthy, A. (1983) Market place participants: A case study of Acharapakkam weekly market, *Proceedings of All India Symposium on Impact of Weekly Markets on Rural Societies*, Geography Department, Madurai University, October 7-10.

Rao, B.P. (1966) Internal and external relations of the port of Vishakhapatnam, *The National Geographical Journal of India*, 2(2).

Rao, B.P. (1967) The study of the port of Cochin, *Geographical Thoughts*, 3(2).

Rao, B.P. (1969) Traffic structure of minor ports of India, *Uttar Bharat Bhugol Patrika*, 5(2), 94-103.

Rao, B.P. (1971) *Vishakhapatnam - A Study in Geography of Port-Town*, The National Geographical Society of India.

Rao, H.S.G. and Maheswari, A. (1985) Whither central wholesale markets ?, in *Agricultural Markets in Semi- Arid Tropics*, Patancheru, International Crop Research Institute for the Semi-Arid Tropics, 147-152.

Rao, K.V.S. *et al.* (1984) A study on impact of regulated markets and roads on productivity and market arrivals in Andhra Pradesh, *Proceedings of National Workshop on Regulation and Management of Agricultural Produce Markets at Jaipur*, Rajasthan, February.

Rao, K.V.S., Oppen von M. and Parathasarathy, Rao, P. (1985) Impact of market access on agricultural productivity in India, *Proceedings of International Workshop on Agricultural Markets in the Semi-Arid Tropics*, Patancheru, International Crop Research Institute for the Semi-Arid Tropics, October.

Rao, M.S. and Kannan, M. (1983) Location characteristics and distribution of weekly markets in Ramanathapuram district, Tamil Nadu, *Proceedings of All India Symposium on Impact of Weekly Markets on Rural Societies*, Geography Department, Madurai University, October 7-10.

Rao, P.P. (1985) Marketing of fodder in rural and uran areas of India, in *Agricultural Markets in the Semi-Arid Tropics*, Patancheru, International Crop Research Institute for the Semi-Arid Tropics, 97-108.

Rao, P.P. and Rao, T.R. (1972) Criteria for selection of market towns in India, in *Markets Towns and Spatial development*, National Council of Applied Economic Research, 119-20.

Rao, P.P. and Verhagen, H.M.W.J. (1985) Marketing channels of commercial farm inputs in Semi-Arid Tropical India, *Proceedings of International Conference on Commercial Activities and Rural Development*, Geography Department, Gorakhpur University, December 23-25.

Rao, R. (1959) *Regulated Markets in India with Special Reference to Andhra Pradesh*, Unpublished Ph. D. Dissertation, Allahabad University.

Rao, T.V.S. and Subramanyam, E.V.R.S. (1985) Interlocking of credit and product markets and its impact on agricultural productivity, in *Agricultural Markets in the Semi-Arid Tropic*, Patancheru, International Crop Research Institute for the Semi-Arid Tropics, 159-68.

Rathore, N.S. (1979) *Regulated Markets in Rajasthan - A Critical Study in Organisation and Working*, Unpublished Ph. D. Dissertation, Geography Department, Udaipur University.

Raza, M. (1971) Structure and function of rural markets in tribal Bihar, *The Geographer*, 18(1), 17-24.

Raza, M. (ed.) (1979) *A Survey of Research in Geography (1969-72)*, Bombay-New Delhi, Allied Publishers for the Indian Council of Social Science Research.

Raza, M. *et al.* (1980) Economic base and commodity flows - A case study of the Indian urban system, *The National Geographical Journal of India*, 26(3-4).

Reddy, N.V. (1972) Market towns and spatial development in India - A case study of Rayalseema, in *Market Towns and Spatial development*, New Delhi, National Council of Applied Economic Research, 152-54.

Reddy, S.N. (1961) Vegetable markets and regional relationships of Hyderabad city, *Geographical Review of India*, 23(3), 81-99.

Sami, A. (1974) Retail Structure of Patna, *Indian Geographical Studies*, 3, 69-78.

Sami, A. (1975a) Growth and commercial structure of population, *Indian Geographical Studies*, 4.

Sami, A. (1975b) Trend and growth of commercial landuse,*Indian Geographical Studies*, 5, 34-42.

Sami, A. (1975-76) *Functional Spatial Analysis of Patna*, Unpublished Ph. D. Dissertation, Geography Department, Patna University.

Sami, A. (1976) Evolution of commercial centres in Patna, *Indian Geographical Studies*, 7.

Sami, A. (1978) Changes in commercial functions in Patna, *Indian Geographical studies*, 10.

Sami, A. (1980a) Delimitation of retail centres - A case study of Patna, *Indian Geographical Studies*, 14.

Sami, A. (1980b) The geography of retailing - A conceptual review, in R.B. Mandal and V.N.P. Sinha (eds.) *Recent Trends and Concepts in Geography*, Vol. 2, New Delhi, Concept Publishing Company, 151-69.

Sami, A. (1980c) *Intra-Urban Market Geography*, New Delhi, Concept Publishing Company.

Saharia, R.B. and Mathur, B.B. (1984) Morphology of market places of Moradabad town, *The Indian Journal of Marketing Geography*, 2(1-2), 88-93.

Sarkar, A.K. (1972) Role of market centres and regulated marketing in the development process, in *Market Towns and Spatial Development*, New Delhi, National Council of Applied Economic Research, 145-46.

Saxena, H.M. (1971) *Geography of Transport and Market Centres - A Case Study of Hadaoti Plateau*, Unpublished Ph. D. Dissertation, Geography Department, Udaipur University.

Saxena, H.M. (1972) A geographical study of the fairs of Hadaoti Plateau, *The Deccan Geographer*, 10(1), 65- 69.

Saxena, H.M. (1974) Kota - A case study in market morphology, *Geographical Review of India*, 36(1), 45-49.

Saxena, H.M. (1975) *Geography of Transport and Market Centres - A Case Study of Hadaoti Plateau*, New Delhi, S. Chand & Co.

Saxena, H.M. (1977) Marketing geography - A review, *The Deccan Geographer*, 15(1), 250-60.

Saxena, H.M. (1979) Morphology of market towns - Theoretical aspects and a case study of Sriganganagar, *Geographical Outlook*, 14, 87-93.

Saxena, H.M. (1980a) Consumer behaviour - Space perception in retail marketing - A case study of Sriganganagar town, *Geographical Aspects, Rajasthan Geographical Conference*, 74-78.

Saxena, H.M. (1980b) Marketing geography - Concepts and trends, in R.B. Mandal and V.N.P. Sinha (eds.) *Recent Trends and Concepts in Geography*, Vol. 2, New Delhi, Concept Publishing Company, 141-49.

Saxena, H.M. (1980c) *Geographical Study of Market Towns in Rajasthan*, Unpublished ICSSR Research Project, New Delhi, Indian Council of Social Science Research.

Saxena, H.M. (1982) Rural markets - A perspective for development, *Annals of the Association of Rajasthan Geographers*, 2, 31-34.

Saxena, H.M. (1983a) Commodity structure of market towns in Rajasthan, *The Indian Journal of Marketing Geography*, 1(1-2), 19-21.

Saxena, H.M. (1983b) Delimitation of trade areas of market towns in Rajasthan, *Geographical Review of India*, 45(3), 40-45.

Saxena, H.M. (1984) *Geography of Marketing*, New Delhi, Sterling Publishers.

Saxena, H.M. (1985) Rural market place exchange system in Rajasthan, *Proceedings of International Conference on Commercial Activities and Rural Development*, Geography Department, Gorakhpur University, December 23-25.

Selvam, L.G. (1972) Planning and development of market towns, in *Market Towns and Spatial Development*, New Delhi, National Council of Applied Economic Research, 83-84.

Setharam, K. and Chakraborty, S.C. (1979) Further considerations on inter-regional commodity movement in India, *Indian Journal of Regional Sciencs*, 2(1).

Shafi, M. (1972) Geography of transport and marketing, in *A Survey of Research in Geography*, Bombay, Popular Prakashan, 84-95 and 361-62.

Shafi, M. (1980) Regional distribution of cereals and livestock in the Islamic World, *The Geographer*, 27(1).

Shah, S.M. (1972) Pilot research project in growth centres, in *Market Towns and Spatial Development*, New Delhi, National Council of Applied Economic Research, 149-51.

Shantha Kumari, A. (1983) Trichy district - A study on locational characteristics and rural weekly markets, *Proceedings of All India Symposium on Impact of Weekly Markets on Rural Societies*, Geography Department, Madurai University, October 7-10.

Sharma, B.D. (1976) Administrative aspects of marketing in tribal areas, *Indian Journal of Public Administration*, 22(3),403-29.

Sharma, N. (1985) Reorganizing commercial complexes: A case mechanism of rural growth process, *Proceedings of International Conference on Commercial Activities and Rural Development* Geography Department, Gorakhpur University, December 23-25.

Sharma, P.K. (1983) *Market Centres in Central Assam - A Geographi-*

cal Analysis, Unpublished Ph. D. Dissertation, Geography Department, Utkal University.

Sharma, P.K. and Singh, D.K. (1984) Spatial analysis of hierarçhy of market centres and domestic market potential surface of central Assam, *The Indian Journal of Marketing Geography*, 2(1-2), 45-64.

Sharma, R.C. and Kumar, A. (1981) Spatial organization of market facilities - A case study of Kannauj block, *Transactions - Indian Council of Geographers*, 9.

Sharma, S.C. (1985) Spatio-temporal changes in the cultivation of commercial crops in the Tarai tract of eastern U.P., *Proceedings of International Conference on Commercial Activities and Rural Development*, Geography Department, Gorakhpur University, December 23-25.

Sharma, S.K. and Archana (1980) Influence of market factor on agricultural landuse, *The Geographer*, 27(1).

Shasmal, K.C. (1977) Gosaba - A rural market in the Sundarbans, West Bengal, *Folklore*, 18(5), 164-72.

Shukla, S.K. (1985) Role of commercial activities in the process of rural development - A case study of Sagar region, *Proceedings of International Conference on Commercial Activities and Rural Development*, Geography Department, Gorakhpur University, December 23-25.

Sikder, B.P. (1985) Marketing of fertilizers and other inputs for rainfed agriculture, in *Agricultural Markets in Semi-Arid Tropics*, Patancheru, International Crop Research Institute for the Semi-Arid Tropics, 21-28.

Singh, A. (1967) Local business activities index, *Journal of Regional Science*, 7.

Singh, A.J. (1972) Location of regulated markets in Punjab, in*Market Towns and Spatial Development*, New Delhi, National Council of Applied Economic Research, 166-70.

Singh D.K. and Routray, R.K. (1985) Rural market potential as a measure in regional development, *Proceedings of International Conference on Commercial Activities and Rural Development*, Geography Department, Gorakhpur University, December 23-25.

Singh, H. et al. (1965) Kurali market - A report on the economic geography of marketing in northern Punjab, *Economic Development and Cultural Change*, 13, 129-68.

Singh, J. (1975) Grain markets for Bihar held-up land acquisition hurdle, *Times of India*, July 15, 7-8.

Singh, J. (1978) Consumer travel pattern in a backward economy - Gorakhpur region, *The National Geographical Journal of India*, 24(3-4).

Singh, J. (1979) Geography of transport and marketing, in *A Survey of Research in Geography (1969-72)*, New Delhi, Indian Council of Social Science Research.

Singh, J.P. (1975) Hierarchy of business structure in Shillong, *Indian Geographical Studies*, 4.

Singh, J.P. (1980) Commercial structure of Shillong, *Geographical Review of India*, 42(1).

Singh, K.N. (1961) Barhaj - A study in the changing pattern of a market town, *The National Geographical Journal of India*, 7(1), 21-36.

Singh, K.N. (1963) *Rural Markets and Rurban Centres in Eastern Uttar Pradesh - A Geographical Analysis*, Unpublished Ph. D. Dissertation, Geography Department, Banaras Hindu University.

Singh, L.R. (1980a) *Recent Trends in Indian Geography*, Presidential Address, Silver Jubilee Session, Indian Council of Geographers.

Singh L.R. (1980b) Spatial aspects of periodic markets and regulated market systems in India - A case study, *Proceedings of Asian Regional Evalution Workshop*, Bangalore, 1-20.

Singh, L.R. (1983) Spatial planning of rural markets, in India, *National geographer*, 18(2), 193-204.

Singh, L.R. (1985) Spatial organization and planning of agricultural markets in U.P. India, *Proceedings of the Fourth National Workshop on Agricultural Markets*, Lucknow.

Singh, L.R. and Dixit, R.S. (1980) Hierarchy of market centres in the umland of Kanpur, *Proceedings of IGU Working Group on Market Place Exchange System,Workshop*, Nagoya.

Singh, L.R. and Dixit, R.S. (1982) *Typology of Market Centres*, Allahabad, G.B.P. Social Science Institute.

Singh, L.R. and Dixit, R.S. (1986) Role of market centres in regional development, in L.R. Singh (ed.) *Regional Planning and Rural Development*, Allahabad, Thinkers' Library.

Singh, L.R. and Lal V.N. (1983) *Wholesale Vegetable and Fruit Market of Khuldabad (Allahabad City) - Retrospect and Prospect*, Allahabad, G.B.P. Social Science Institute.

Singh, L.R. and Sibou, S. (1984) Place of commercial structure in urban morphology - A case study, *The Indian Journal of Geography*, 14, 1-32.

Singh, M. (1984) Rural markets and marketing functions - Case Studies from lower Ganga-Ghaghara Doab, *The Indian Journal of Marketing Geography*, 2(1-2), 94-97.

Singh, R.B. and Singh, K.K. (1976) Maya Bazar - Geographical study of a rural service centre, *Uttar Bharat Bhugol Patrika*, 12(2), 92-101.

Singh, R.L. and Singh, R.P.B. (1977) Spatial and structural analysis of the rural market network and its relation to society in an Indian environment, *The National Geographical Journal of India*, 22(3-4), 151-59.

Singh, S.B. (1982) Periodic markets and rural development - A case study, *The National Geographical Journal of India*, 28(1-2), 86-92.

Singh, S.K. (1972) Role of electricity in the development of a market town - Lar (Deoria) - A case study, *The National Geographical Journal of India*, 18(1), 5-17.

Singh, S.M. (1958) *Rural Markets and Urban Settlements in the District of Faizabad*, Unpublished M.A. Dissertation, Geography Department, Banaras Hindu University.

Singh, S.M. (1965) The stability theory of rural central place development, *The National Geographical Journal of India*, 11(1), 13-21.

Singh, U. (1959) Growth of transport and commerce in Allahabad, *The National Geographical Journal of India*, 4(4).

Singh, U. (1960) Industrial and commercial landscape of Allahabad city, *The National Geographical Journal of India*, 4(4), 227-41.

Singhal, R.C. (1979) Developing market facilities: The rural markets under SF/MF and AL Programme, *Economic Affairs*, 24(10-12), 269-71.

Sinha, B.N. (1974) *Trade and Industrial Market of Bihar*, Patna, Arvind Publications.

Sinha, B.N. (ed.) (1983) Progress of Geographical Research in India, *Transactions - Indian Council of Geographers*, 11.

Sinha, B.N. (ed.) (1984) Progress of Geographical Research in India, *Transactions - Indian Council of Geographers*, 13.

Sinha, B.N. (ed.) (1986) *Trends in Geographical Research in India*, Bhubaneswar, Indian Council of Geographers.

Sinha, B.R.K. (1985) Human resources utilization in Commercial activities in rural area - A case study of Dhanaura block (District Patna), *Proceedings of International Conference on Commercial Activities and Rural Development*, Geography Department, Gorakhpur University, December 23-25.

Sinha, D.P. (1963) The Role of Phariya in tribal acculturation in a central Indian Market, *Ethnology*, 2(2), 170-79.

Sinha, D.P. (1964) *The Role of Banari-Intertribal Market Among the Hill People of Chhota Nagpur - A Study in Cultural Change*, Unpublished Ph.D. Dissertation, South Illinois University.

Sinha, D.P. (1968) *Culture Change in an Inter-tribal Market*, Bombay, Asia Publishing House.

Sinha, M.K. (1968) *Spatial Distribution of Retail Trade - A Case Study of Patna*, Unpublished M.C.P. Dissertation, Kharagpur, Indian Institute of Technology.

Sinha, S. (1951) Weekly market at Bamnia in Manbhum, *The Geographical Review of India*, 13(4).

Sinha, S. (1961) The market at Bamnia, *Bulletin of the Anthropological Survey of India*, 10(1).

Sinha, V.N.P. and Mandal, R.B. (1974) Hierarchy of trade towns in Bihar, *Indian Geographical Studies*, 3, 79-84.

Sita, K. (1976) Periodic markets - A study in south Konkan *Geographical Outlook*, 12.

Sivamurthy, A. and Ramaswamy, G. (1983) The structure of Acharapakkam weekly market, *Proceedings of All India Symposium on Impact of Weekly Markets on Rural Societies*, Geography Department, Madurai University, October 7-10.

Srivastava, H.O. (1980) *Geography of Market Centres in Saryupar Plain, U.P.*, Unpublished Ph. D. Dissertation, Geography Department, Gorakhpur University.

Srivastava, H.O. (1984) Spatio-temporal synchronization of market centres in Saryupar Plain, *The Indian Journal of Marketing Geography*, 2(1-2), 40-44.

Srivastava, H.O. (1985) The nature of market area regions in Saryupar Plain, *Proceedings of International Conference on Commercial Activities and Rural Development*, Geography Department, Gorakhpur University, December 23-35.

Srivastava, H.O. and Srivastava, V.K. (1980) The hierarchy of rural market centres - A methodological approach, *The Deccan Geographer*, 18(2), 815-21.

Srivastava, K.R. (1974) A model for the study of an individual market place, *Uttar Bharat Bhugol Patrika*, 10(1-2), 80-87.

Srivastava, K.R. (1976) Spatial distribution of rural markets in Meerut district, *Uttar Bharat Bhugol Patrika*, 12(1), 12-15.

Srivastava, K.R. (1983) *Periodic Markets and Central Places in*

Baghelkhand Region, Unpublished Ph. D. Dissertation, Geography Department, Jabalpur University.

Srivastava, K.R. and Srivastava, V.K. (1984) Geographical personality of a rural market of Indian Tarai, *The Indian Journal of Marketing Geography*, 2(1-2), 82-87.

Srivastava, R.C. (1985) Marketing systems and problems in the Patha area of Bundelkhand, U.P., *Proceedings of International Conference on Commercial Activities and Rural Development*, Geography Department, Gorakhpur University, December 23-25.

Srivastava, R.C. and Gupta, J.P. (1979) Consumer travel patterns of the periodic markets of Kanpur metropolis, *National Geographer*, 14(2).

Srivastava, V.K. (1971) Trade centres in the upper Son Basin, *Research Journal of Gorakhpur University*, 37-42.

Srivastava, V.K. (1976a) Locational compatibility of trade centres in Baghelkhand Plateau, in V.C. Misra *et al.* (eds.) *Essays in Applied Geography*, Sagar University, 259-68.

Srivastava, V.K. (1976b) Market periodicity and centrality - A methodological approach, *Mainzer Geographische Studien*, Heft 10, 33-38.

Srivastava, V.K. (1977) Periodic markets and rural development - Bahraich district - A case study, *National Geographer*, 12(1), 47-55.

Srivastava, V.K. (1978) Theoretical norms and interpretations of market place participants' behaviour, *National Geographer*, 13(2), 117-24.

Srivastava, V.K. (1981) Agricultural markets of U.P., in N. Mohd. (ed.) *Perspectives in Agricultural Geography*, Vol. 3, New Delhi, Concept Publishing Company.

Srivastava, V.K. (1982) *Geography of Market Centres in the Tarai Region of U.P.*, Project Report Unpublished, New Delhi, Indian Council of Social Science Research.

Srivastava, V.K. (1983a) Morphology of rural markets around Gorakhpur town, *The Indian Journal of Marketing Geography*, 1(1-2), 28-38.

Srivastava, V.K. (1983b) Rural marketing and social structure in north India, in C.R. Pathak (ed.) *Urban and Regional Change in Developing Countries*, Calcutta.

Srivastava, V.K. (ed.) (1983c) *Market Studies*, The Association of Geographers of India, 1(1-2).

Srivastava, V.K. (1984a) Progress of marketing geography in India,

The Indian Journal of Marketing Geography, 2(1-2), 1-13.

Srivastava, V.K. (1984b) Socio-economic hierarchy of markets in north India, *Geographical Review of India*, 46(1).

Srivastava, V.K. (1984c) Market place trade systems and socio-economic patterns of populations, *Proceedings of IGU Symposium on Market Place Exchange System*, France, August.

Srivastava, V.K. (ed.) (1984d) *The Indian Journal of Marketing Geography*, The Association of Geographers of India, 2(1-2).

Srivastava, V.K. (1985a) Behavioural characteristics of market place participants in the Tarai region of U.P., in *Agricultural Markets in the Semi-Arid Tropics*, Patancheru, International Crop Research Institute for the Semi-Arid Tropics, 153.

Srivastava, V.K. (1985b) Geography of commercial activities - A trend report, *Proceedings of International Conference on Commercial Activities and Rural Development*, Geography Department, Gorakhpur University, December 23-25.

Srivastava, V.K. (1987) *Geography of Marketing and Rural Development*, New Delhi, Inter-India Publications.

Srivastava, V.K. (ed.) (1988) *Commercial Activities and Rural Development in South Asia*, New Delhi, Concept Publishing Company.

Srivastava, V.K. and Nayak, H.P. (1980) Origin and development of market centres, *Uttar Bharat Bhugol Patrika*, 16(2), 117-26.

Srivastava, V.K. and Rai, J.P. (1978) Hierarchy of market centres - A methodological approach, *Uttar Bharat Bhugol Patrika*, 14(2), 97-104.

Srivastava, V.K. and Srivastava, H.O. (1979) Distributional pattern and classification of market centres in the Saryupar Plain, *The Deccan Geographer*, 17(1), 516-23.

Subbarao, K. (1985) Institutions, infra-structure and regional variations in India's input delivery system, in *Agricultural Markets in the Semi-Arid Tropics*, Patancheru, International Crop Research Institute for the Semi-Arid Tropics, 29-40.

Subbiah, S. (1983) Ecological complex and evolution of periodic market places in Tamil Nadu - A case study from Tiruchirapalli district, *Proceedings of All India Symposium on Impact of Weekly Markets on Rural Societies*, Geography department, Madurai University, October 7-10.

Subbiah, S. (1984) Exploring the ecological complex model towards an understanding of evolution of peasant markets in a semi-arid ecology - A case study of Tamil Nadu, India, *Proceedings - IGU Symposium on Market Place Exchange Systems*, France, August.

Sur, S. (1985) Periodic markets and social integration, *Indian Journal of Regional Science*, 12(2), 1-16.

Surat, R. (1985) Commercial characteristics of agricultural mandies A case study of eastern U.P., *Proceedings of International Conference on Commercial Activities and Rural Development*. Geography Department, Gorakhpur University, December 23-25.

Suresh, R. (1971) Parade - A periodical market of Kanpur. *The Geographical Knowledge*, 4, 56-65.

Suri, K.B. (1972) Growth of small towns in India A comparative study of rapidly growing and declining towns, in *Market Towns and Spatial Development*, National Council of Applied Economic Research, 93-95.

Swami, M.R.K. *et al.* (1982) Rural marketing service centres, Jangam, *SEDME*, 9(4) December, 253-63.

Swami, P. (1942) Kumbha mela, *The Indian Geographical Journal*, 17(2).

Swaminathan, E. (1976) *Market Centres and Consumer Preference within Coimbatore Metropolitan Area*, Unpublished Ph. D. Dissertation, Geography Department, Madras University.

Swaminathan, E. (1983a) Comparative study of weekly markets in Coimbatore and Madurai districts in Tamil Nadu, *Proceedings of All India Symposium on Impact of Weekly Markets on Rural Societies*, Geography Department, Madurai University, October 7-10.

Swaminathan, E. (1983b) A study on the locational characteristics of weekly markets in Madurai district, *Proceedings of All India Symposium on Impact of Weekly Markets on Rural Societies*, Geography Department, Madurai University, October 7-10.

Swaminathan, E. (1985) Market centres and their hierarchy in Coimbatore region, Tamil Nadu, *Proceedings of International Conference on Commercial Activities and Rural Development*, Geography Department, Gorakhpur university, December 23-25.

Swaminathan, E. and Murugesan, N. (1984) Functional morphology and market place participants' behaviour in Pudansandai weekly market, *The Indian Journal of Marketing Geography*, 2(1-2), 35-39.

Talwar, B.R. (1972) Market towns in Punjab, in *Market Towns and Spatial Development*, New Delhi. National Council of Applied

Economic Research, 201-03.

Tamaskar, B.G. (1955) Patharia Kalan - A study of the settlement pattern and weekly market, *Geographical Review of India*, 17(4), 1-12.

Tamaskar, B.G. (1965) The cattle fair at Garhakota, *Geographical Magazine*, 18(1).

Tamaskar, B.G. (1966a) The weekly markets of Sagar-Damoh Plateau, *The National Geographical Journal of India*, 12(1), 38-50.

Tamaskar, B.G. (1966b) The fair centres of Sagar-Damoh Plateau, *Nagpur University Journal*, 17(1).

Tamaskar, B.G. (1977) Periodic marketing system in medieval Maharashtra, *Geographical Review of India*, 39(2), 173-82.

Tamaskar, B.G. (1978) Geographical perspectives on periodic marketing system and network in the Chhattisgarh Plain, *Geographical Review of India*, 40(1), 15-24.

Tamaskar, B.G. (1979a) The marketing efficiency of periodic marketing system and network, *Indian Journal of Landscape System and Ecological Studies*, 2(1-2).

Tamaskar, B.G. (1979b) Fair centres of Chhattisgarh Plain, *National Geographer*, 14(1), 55-70.

Tamaskar, B.G. (1979c) The livestock marketing system in Chhattisgarh Plain, *The Journal of North-East India Geographical Society*, 11(1-2).

Tamaskar, B.G. (1979d) *The Periodic Marketing System and Network Project on the Arvi Upland*, Unpublished Research Project, New Delhi, University Grants Commission.

Tamaskar, B.G. (1981) Market attractiveness of Arvi Upland, *Geographical Review of India*, 43(4).

Tamaskar, B.G. (1983a) Stability and persistence of periodic market places in urban centres, *Indian Journal of Landscape System and Ecological Studies*, 6(1-2).

Tamaskar, B.G. (1983b) Trader travel behaviour and periodic market cycles in the Arvi Upland, *Market Studies*, 1(1-2).

Tamaskar, B.G. (1984a) Indian fair centre system and networks, *Vikas Sheel Bhugol Patrika*, 3(1-2), 32-41.

Tamaskar, B.G. (1984b) The role of periodic market places as centres of diffusion, *The Deccan Geographer*, 22(3), 519-25.

Tamaskar, B.G. (1985a) Marketing system on the Arvi Upland, *The Deccan Geographer*, 23(1), 555-71.

Tamaskar, B.G. (1985b) Economic functions of weekly market places,

Proceedings of International Conference on Commercial Activities and Rural Development, Geography Department, Gorakhpur University, December 23-25.

Tamaskar, B.G. and Gedam, D.A. (1983) Typology of service areas of periodic marketing system and network, *Transactions - Indian Institute of Geographers*, 5(1).

Thakur, B. (1968) The CBD of Patna, Proceedings of Symposium on Urban Landuse, *Proceedings IGU Congress*, Hyderabad.

Thakur, B. (1974) Models of intra-urban consumer travel behaviour, *Indian Geographical Studies*, 2, 21-27.

Thygarajan, V. (1940) Port of Tuticorin, *Journal of Madras Geographical Association*, 15(4).

Tiwari, R.C. and Lal, M. (1985) Spatial planning of rural market centres in Rai-Bareli District U.P., *Proceedings of International Conference on Commercial Activities and Rural Development*, Geography Department, Gorakhpur University, December 23-25.

Tiwari, R.C. and Lal, M. (1986) Rural markets in Rai-Bareli district, *Geographical Review of India*, 48(3), 29-37.

Tiwari, R.C. and Tripathi, S. (1984) Vipnan bhugol, *Bhu Sangam*, 2(1), 45-56.

Tripathi, V.B. and Chand, R. (1983) Micro-level locational planning for market facilities - A case study of Bulandshahr district, *The Geographer*, 30(2).

Twade, M.D. and Gophane, B.N. (1985) Marketing organization and commercial fruit farming - The case of Konkan, *Proceedings of International Conference on Commercial Activities and Rural Development*, Geography Department, Gorakhpur University, December 23-25.

Uppal, J.S. (1978) Role of regulated markets, *Kurukshetra*, 26(7), 17-18.

Uppal, J.S. (1979) Vridhachalam market in south Arcot district, Tamil Nadu State, India, in *Rural Markets: A Critical Link for Small Farmer Development*, Food and Agricultural Organization Bangkok, 143-60.

Vasudeo, Rao D. (1980) Distribution of weekly markets and rural development, *Eastern Economist*, 75(16), 907-909.

Veeranna, S. (1963) Planning of shopping facilities in towns and cities, *Journal of the Institute of Town Planning*.

Velayanathan, S. (1983) Rural weekly markets and spatial interaction pattern of consumers in Madurai Metropolitan Area, *Proceedings of All India Symposium on Impact of Weekly Markets on Rural Societies*, Geography Department, Madurai University, October 7-10.

Vepa, R.K. (1972) Small towns as levers of industrial growth in rural areas, in *Market Towns and Spatial Development*, New Delhi, National Council of Applied Economic Research, 79-82.

Venugopal, V. (1972) Commercial structure of Warangal city in Andhra Pradesh, *Proceedings of the IGU Symposium on Urban Landuse*, Hyderabad.

Verghese, I. (1971) Weekly markets in a Mysore town, *Journal of Indian Anthropological Society*, 6(2), 107-18.

Verma, L.N. and Saxena, H.M. (1968) Jhalrapatan - A geographical study of a market centre, *The Deccan Geographer*, 6(2), 25-36.

Verma, R.D. (1987) *Analysis of Periodic Market Centres in Pratapgarh District U.P.*, Unpublished Ph. D. Dissertation, Geography Department, Kanpur University.

Verma, R.V. (1980) Role of periodic markets in integrated area development - A case study of Safipur Tehsil of Unnao district, U.P., *Transactions - Indian Council of Geographers*, 8.

Verma, S.C. (1980) Developing rural markets for small farmers, *Kurukshetra*, 28(9), 14-18.

Verma, S.C. (1985) Public interventions in agricultural markets in India, in *Agricultural Markets in the Semi-Arid Tropics*, Patancheru, International Crop Research Institute for the Semi-Arid Tropics, 328-34.

Vishwanath, M.S. (1966-67) *A Geographical Analysis of Rural Markets and Rurban Centres in Mysore*, Unpublished Ph.D. Dissertation, Geography Department, Banaras Hindu University.

Vishwanath, M.S. (1972) Establishment and development of rurban centres, in *Market Towns and Spatial Development*, New Delhi, National Council of Applied Economic Research, 147-48.

Vishwanath, V.V. (1979) Growth and development of wholesale grain and vegetable markets of Madras city, *Transactions - Institute of Indian Geographers*, 1(1).

Vishwanath, V.V. (1979b) *Functional Analysis of Wholesale Marketing of Foodgrains and Vegetables in Madras City*, Unpublished Ph. D. Dissertation, Geography Department, Madras University.

Wanmali, S. (1976) Market centres and distribution of consumer goods in rural India - A case study of Singhbhum district, south Bihar, *Mainzer Geographische Studien*, Heft, 10, 49-56.

Wanmali, S. (1978) *Periodic Markets in South Bihar*, Unpublished Ph. D. Dissertation, Geography Department, University of Cambridge.

Wanmali, S. (1979) The regulated and periodic systems of marketing of agricultural produce and their impact on rural development, *Proceedings of the Third Indo-British Geography Seminar*, Madras, Tirupati, and Mysore, December 8-17.

Wanmali, S. (1980) The regulated and periodic markets and rural development in India, *Institute of British Geographers' Transactions*, 5(4), 466-86.

Wanmali, S. (1980-81) *Periodic Markets and Rural Development in India - A Case Study of Singhbhum District*, Bihar, New Delhi, Concept Publishing Company.

Wanmali, S. (1983) *Service Provision and Rural Development in India - A Case Study of Miryal Guda Taluk*, Research Project Report, No. 37, Washington D.C., International Food Research Institue.

Wanmali, S. (1985) Network of distribution of goods and services in rural India: Some spatial considerations, in *Agricultural Markets in the Semi-Arid Tropics*, Patancheru International Crop Research Institute for the Semi-Arid Tropics, 133-38.

Wanmali, S. and Oppen von, M. and Subba Rao, K.V. *et al.* (1982) Equity and efficiency effects of market access for farmers in two regions of India, *Proceedings of International Conference on Improving Geographical Accessibility of Rural Services*, Bangalore, Indian Institute of Management, July.

Warrior, S.K. (1972) Some problems of a public marketing agency and their impact on the marketing development programme, in *Market Towns and Spatial Developments*, New Delhi, National Council of Applied Economic Research, 75-78.

SECTION C

EPILOGUE

12

OVERVIEW OF THE WORK

The present work has presented the inventory of literature on the sub-field of geography of marketing and commercial activities in India. The inventory comprises the inventories (done so far) on the literature in the form of reviews, bibliographies on the one hand, while the literature available in the form of research books, monographs, research project reports, research papers, and abstracts of papers on various perspectives of marketing within geography on the other.

It is important to note that certain very pertinent points have come up from the overview of the on-going research work on geography of marketing and commercial activities in the country.

REVIEWS AND BIBLIOGRAPHIES ON LITERATURE: *THE WORLD CONTEXT*

W. Applebaum, R.E. Murphy, R.J. Bromley, and R.H.T. Smith have presented notable works on literature of marketing geography at the international level. Through his varied studies, Applebaum dedicated himself to give rise to this field of study as a separate branch of geography. Murphy made it clear that marketing geography had established itself and that it has to be (or rather, must be) realized/recognized. Following the inspirations, varied studies were undertaken and completed all over the world. After 20 years of growth and development, Bromley made valuable contributions (followed by Symanski, Smith, Gormsen and others) to the branch of geography of marketing and commercial activities by presenting bibliographies on the subject in the international context. Gormsen and others also contributed to this area of study on the line of making bibliographies at the regional levels.

There has, however, been a major lacuna in this direction in the sense that no one in India came forward to prepare an inventory of the available literature on the subject. If one wants to step forward, it is very significant that one takes stock of things already available. The project, one in hand, is an humble effort to fillin the said gap.

REVIEWS AND BIBLIOGRAPHIES ON LITERATURE: *THE INDIAN CONTEXT*

The list of reviews etc. in the Indian context reveals that there are 25 documents presented by researchers highlighting the existing treasure of literature on marketing geography in the country. The related chronological table makes it obvious that 3 attempts were made during the 1970s while as many as 22 efforts have been made during the present decade. B.N. Sinha, V.K. Srivastava, H.M. Saxena, and R.S. Dixit have shown keen interest in this context. The ICSSR has undertaken such endeavours while presenting 'Survey' of research in geography from time to time (i.e. 1972, 1979, 1984). Besides, the Concept Publishing Co. has brought out a directory of scholars in various subfields of geography including marketing geography.

RESEARCH BOOKS AND MONOGRAPHS BY INDIAN SCHOLARS

As many as 41 books containing literature on marketing geography have come out in the country during 1930 - 1987. The chronological analysis makes it evident that during this period the decade-wise outcome has been as follows: 1930s-- 2; 1950s-- 3; 1960s-- 3; 1970s-- 15; and 1980s-- 17. One work is undated. Thus, the 1970s and the 1980s are of great significance in this regard. Although, the work started from the 1930s but only 2 books which have been completed during this decade have been traced while during the 1950s and the 1960s, a total of 6 (i.e. 3+3) were brought out. It is also noteworthy that two organizations, the ICSSR, New Delhi and the NCAER, New Delhi have contributed to this area of study by presenting valuable volumes on literature on geography of marketing and commercial activities in the country.

RESEARCH BOOKS AND MONOGRAPHS: *OTHERS ON INDIAN PERSPECTIVES*

Some other researchers have also shown their interest in taking up research projects on issues relating to marketing perspectives of India. In this connection, the names of H. Ishihara and B. Harriss are noteworthy. On the chronological basis, the 1970s and the 1980s are worth mention. Out of a total of 29 works, only 2 belong to the period earlier to 1970s while 9 belong to the 1970s. The 1980s, on the other hand, have an outcome of 18 works.

The total number of research books and monographs through inclusion of the above, thus, comes to 70 (i.e. 41+29) which is certainly a good number for a beginning like that of the present case.

RESEARCH PROJECT REPORTS:
THE DISSERTATIONS

The observations show that the research scholars have shown keen interest in undertaking doctoral (etc.) projects on marketing perspectives at various research centres of the universities in the country. The chronological results being: 1950s-- 2; 1960s-- 5; 1970s-- 14, and 1980s upto 1987-- 8. Thus, the number of dissertations rapidly increased through the last four decades. It is a very remarkable fact relating to growth and development of such studies in India. The 1970s and the 1980s especially show the signs of rapid progress in the sub-field under review in the country.

RESEARCH PROJECT REPORTS:
OTHER THAN DISSERTATIONS

Besides the research projects leading to university degrees, the researchers in India have shown great interest in undertaking research schemes sponsored by various departments of the State/Union Government and autonomous research institutes. Twelve such reports have been traced by the author, the chronological break-up of which is as follows: 1960s-- 2; 1970s-- 3; 1980s-- 7. It is also obvious that although the work in this direction started from the 1960s but most of the research projects were undertaken and completed during the 1970s-1980s.

RESEARCH ARTICLES BY INDIAN SCHOLARS

The inventory of the research articles of Indian scholars has been presented in the form of two kinds of thematic typologies - one from the chronological stand-point and the other one from the point of view of major contributors.

The first typology reveals that during the 1930s, 1940s, and 1950s, the number of articles was only 8 each, thus totalling to 24 while during the 1960s, there were 33 articles contributed to marketing geography in the country by the Indian scholars. Further, during the 1970s, the number was 127 while during the 1980s it stood at 214. These break-ups make it crystal clear that the interest of researchers tremendously increased in the context of market studies. Also, another angle of the consideration makes it evident that earlier to the 1960s only 7 of the 16 perspectives were covered under market studies by the researchers while during the 1960s the number of perspectives covered was 15. In the case of the present decade and the 1970s, however, all the 16 perspectives have been covered.

The second typology presents the number of contributions by eminent scholars under the specified 16 perspectives. Keeping in view the individual researchers and their contributions, the first (three) names under each of the 16 themes of market studies are as follows:

1. Role: Dixit, R.S., Srivastava, V.K., Tamaskar, B.G.
2. Origin/Evolution: Dixit, R.S., Tamaskar, B.G./ Sami, A., Srivastava, V.K.
3. Location/Distribution: Dixit, R.S., Tamaskar, B.G./ Srivastava, V.K., Swaminathan, E.
4. Transport Network: Dixit, R.S., Tamaskar, B.G.
5. Typology: Dixit, R.S., Tamaskar, B.G., Srivastava, V.K.
6. Centrality/Hierarchy: Dixit, R.S., Singh, L.R., Srivastava, V.K.
7. Trade Area: Dixit, R.S., Dutta, A.K., Saxena, H.M.
8. Structure/Morphology: Parvathi, C., Sami, A., Saxena, H.M.
9. Consumer/Trader Behaviour: Dixit, R.S., Dutta, A.K., Srivastava, V.K.
10. Synchronization/Rings/Cycles: Dixit, R.S., Srivastava, V.K., Tamaskar, B.G.
11. Traditional Exchange: Tamaskar, B.G., Dixit, R.S., Srivastava, V.K.
12. Urban/Regulated/Modern: Dixit, R.S., Sami, A./Singh, L.R./ Dutta, A.K./Saxena, H.M.
13. Function: Dixit, R.S., Sami, A.
14. Goods/Commodities: Ramakrishna, K.C., Rao, B.P., Singh, U./ Wanmali, S.
15. Planning: Dixit, R.S., Singh, L.R., Wanmali, S.
16. Others: Dixit, R.S., Tamaskar, B.G., Srivastava, V.K.

In all, however, the analysis shows that there are 33 eminent scholars who are credited for major contributions to the 16 specified perspectives of market studies in geography in the country.

RESEARCH ARTICLES: *OTHERS ON INDIAN PERSPECTIVES*

Among the other researchers, credited for contributing valuable research articles on marketing perspectives of geography in India, are B. Harriss, H.G. Bhole, and E.A.J. Johnson. From the stand-point of chronology, the break-ups of the number of articles are: Before 1960s-- 4; 1960s-- 2; 1970s-- 9; 1980s-- 12.

The analysis makes it evident that the 1970s and 1980s have played a great role in the development of geography of marketing in the country.

RESEARCH CONTRIBUTIONS ON INDIAN PERSPECTIVES: *CLASSIFIED*

Under this, the total research contributions on various aspects of marketing geography in the country - whether by Indian scholars or by others - have been classified according to the type/class of the research piece. The analysis of the facts relating to major contributors and their contributions shows that the volume of work produced during the 1970s and 1980s is considerably large in comparison to the earlier decades, and that it is a good sign of development taking place in this sub-field of geography in the country.

AN EXHAUSTIVE BIBLIOGRAPHY

The bibliography presented by the author is quite exhaustive as it comprises all the contributions on marketing geography of the country. The reviews, references, and bibliographies, so far, prepared by the individual researchers/research organizations (institutes etc.) have included a very limited number of entries, for the reason best known only to them.

The present work, however, consists of an exhaustive bibliography containing about 550 entries on the subject under study.

13

PROSPECTIVE PERSPECTIVES

The overview of the inventory of the research work, done so far, on perspectives on marketing geography of India gives rise to several pertinent points: (i) that before the 1960s only a few studies have been made in this sub-field, (ii) that on all the counts (research books, monographs, research project reports, dissertations, and articles) considerable progress has been made since 1960s and more especially during the present decade, (iii) that the number of marketing perspectives covered under studies was also very limited during the 1960s while during the 1970s and the 1980s the coverage was, rather, full (under the present format), and (iv) that there has been a major lacuna all over these decades in the area of inventory/bibliography/documentation of the researches done so far in the country in the sub-field of marketing geography. Further, it is also noted that there are some facets which have attracted many researchers while many facets have attracted only some scholars for research. The facets related to the location and distribution of market centres have attracted the largest number of researchers followed by studies on traditional/periodic marketing (Table 10).

In view of these facts, it is advisable that more studies be undertaken especially on:

(i) Relationship between transport network and market centres,
(ii) Typologies of markets,
(iii) Structure/ Morphology of markets,
(iv) Consumer/Trader behaviour,
(v) Centrality/ Hierarchy,
(vi) Function,
(vii) Sychronization,
(viii) Goods/Commodities,
(ix) Planning perspectives and
(x) Different dimensions of the role of market centres.

TABLE 10: NUMBER OF CONTRIBUTIONS ON VARIOUS THEMES

Sl. No.	*Theme*	*Number*
1.	Location/Distribution	142
2.	Traditional Exchange	136
3.	Others	126
4.	Urban/Regulated/Modern	93
5.	Origin/Evolution	85
6.	Trade Area	81
7.	Role	78
8.	Planning	71
9.	Goods/Commodities	66
10.	Consumer/Trader Behaviour	43
11.	Synchronization/Cycle/Ring	43
12.	Function	43
13.	Centrality/Hierarchy	41
14.	Structure/Morphology	41
15.	Typology	39
16.	Transport Network	35

Although the research articles are being contributed to the sub-field of marketing geography in good number, there is an imperative need that more and more research project reports based on first hand information/field work and on different types of marketing activities be undertaken/completed through dissertations etc. The findings, further, be published to benefit all the individuals/agencies - governmental and non-governmental in general and the specialists of marketing geography in particular.

The objective of promoting research on market studies can be achieved by the establishment of various research organizations at the national/international level. Besides, academic meets on marketing perspectives should be organized at the national/international level to arouse the interest of researchers on the one hand and to discuss the significant matters and finding out solutions to major issues of marketing research in geography in the country on the other.

At this state, it is noteworthy that some steps have been taken/are being taken in this direction in the country such as:

(a) Increase in Doctoral Dissertations, and Post-Doctoral Reports in progress.

(b) Establishment of Academic Bodies/Organizations.

(c) Organization of Academic Meets on Marketing Geography.

The author has tried to trace out the steps being taken for promotion of research in marketing geography in the geography departments of various Indian universities.

The efforts revealed that more than three dozens of doctoral dissertations and post-doctoral research projects sponsored by the University Grants Commission/Indian Council of Social Science Research are nearly completed in the country. Likewise, some academic bodies have been established at the national/international level and some publications of the same are also out. Besides, some academic meets, i.e. conferences, seminars, symposia, workshops etc. have been organized on market studies and the related proceedings, too, have been or are being brought out. And yet, there is an utmost need to undertake more and more such projects/programmes etc. in this regard.

The details of the above there dimensions are as follows:

DOCTORAL AND POST-DOCTORAL RESEARCH PROJECTS IN PROGRESS

1. Ahmad, I. Geography of Transport and Market Centres in Western U.P., Aligarh University.
2. Banerjee, C. Variations in Insurance Credit Facilities in Rural Development in West Bengal with special reference to Siliguri Naxalbari Area, North Bengal University.
3. Chauhan, K.S. Spatial Aspects of Weekly Markets in Upper Ganga-Yamuna Doab, Aligarh University.
4. Gupta, R.N.P. Spatial Development of Market Centres in Bhagalpur District, Bhagalpur University.
5. Jain, A.K. Marketing in an Agricultural Region - A Geographical Study of Periodic Markets in Vidisa Plateau, M.P., Sagar University.
6. Nayak, H.P. System and Network of Agricultural Market Places in U.P., Avadh University.
7. Patil, B. Weekly Markets in Bijapur District.
8. Sengupta, S.K. Behaviour of Spatial Development in Land Value in Bangalore Metropolitan Area, North Bengal University.
9. Mukhopadhyaya, T. Retail Commercial Structure of Greater Bombay, Bombay University (since 1977).
10. Umamaheswari, P. Wholesale Function of Bombay and its Spa-

tial Linkages, Bombay University (since 1979).

11. Aruna, C.K. Role of Agricultural Market Centres in Urban and Regional Development, Osmania University (since 1980).
12. Jamkar, A.G. The Periodic Marketing System and Network in Dhule District, Nagpur University (since 1980).
13. Padmini, D. Shopping Behaviour of Madras Metropolitan Area, Madras University (since 1980).
14. Yadav, H.R. The Pattern of Retail Locations in Towns of Saryupar Plain, Gorakhpur University (since 1981).
15. Das, P.K. Market Centres and Rural Development in Orissa - A Geographical Analysis, Utkal University. (since 1982).
16. Patil, M.N. Spatial Organization of Agricultural Markets in Marathawada - A Geographical Analysis, Shivaji University (since 1982).
17. Sayed, Z.A. The Rural Tribal Market Area of Dangs District, Baroda University (since 1982).
18. Tiwari, K.N. Market and Transportation - A Case Study in Geography of Marketing of Ghazipur District, U.P., Gorakhpur University (since 1982).
19. Verma, S.R. A Study of Weekly Market Centres of District Saharanpur, Meerut University Completed (1983).
20. Gholag, T.N. Distribution of Livestock and Fodder Supply in Maharashtra, Shivaji University (since 1983).
21. Kumar, B.S. Periodic Markets and Rural Development of Purnia Plain, Banaras Hindu University (since 1983).
22. Nath, T. Marketing Geography of the Urban Fringe of Allahabad, Gorakhpur University (since 1983).
23. Kaur, D. Spatial Organization and Functional Interdependency of Market Centres of Khargone District (West Niwar) in M.P., Rani A.D. University, Indore.
24. Lal, N. Marketing System and Social Structure In Mirzapur District, U.P., Gorakhpur University.
25. Singh, R.S. Geography of Wholesaling - A Case Study of the Agricultural Mandies of Eastern U.P., Gorakhpur University---Completed.
26. Srivastava, M.C. Market Centres and Rural Development in Southern Rajasthan, Vagad Region, Baroda University (since 1983).
27. Ukey, K.A. Cattle Marketing System and Network in Aurangabad District, Nagpur University (since 1983).

28. Wankhedo, S.B. The Periodic Marketing System and Network in Aurangabad District, Nagpur University (since 1983).
29. Yadav, D.P. Marketing Geography of the Urban Fringe of Varanasi, Gorakhpur University (since 1983).
30. Awasthi, N. Market Towns and Spatial Development - A Case Study of Bhopal Region of M.P., Bhopal University (1984) ----Completed.
31. Geetha, T.A. Spatial Analysis of Periodic Markets in Dharampuri District, Madras University (since 1984).
32. Jayaswal, B.L. Geo-Economic Development of Amravati District with Special Reference to Cotton Cultivation and Trade in Post-Independence Period, Nagpur University (since 1984).
33. Reddy, S.N. Periodic Markets and Rural Development - A case Study of Karimnagar District of Andhra Pradesh, Osmania University (since 1984).
34. Singh, A.L. Locational Analysis of Market Centres of Manipur - A Geographical Study, Utkal University (since 1984).
35. Thakure, B.D. Livestock Market Place Exchange System and Network in Nasik District (M.S.) - A Case Study, Nagpur University (since 1984).
36. Rai, J.P. Impact of Rural Market Centres on Rural Development - A Case Study of Lower Son-Basin, U.G.C. Res. Project, D.C.S.K.C. Maunath Bhanjan.
37. Dixit, R.S. Marketing Geography: The Indian Scenario-Inventory and Prospects, ICSSR Post-Doctoral Res. Project, 1988 Completed.
38. Dixit, R.S. Periodic Marketing in an Urban Environment - Mahoba: A Case Study in Geography of Commercial Activities, U.G.C. Post-Doctoral Research Project, Isabella Thoburn College, Lucknow, 1989 Completed.

ACADEMIC BODIES/ORGANIZATIONS

1981: The Association of Marketing Geographers of India, Gorakhpur Organ: Market Studies: The Indian Journal of Marketing Geography, First Volume released at the 5th Indian Geography Congress at Aligarh Muslim University (December 1983).
Second Volume, The Indian Journal of Marketing Geography, International Geographical Union Special Number released in France (August 1984) on the occasion of the 25th International Geographical Congress

of the IGU.
Third Volume (1985) and the Fourth Volume (1986) also released.
Chief Editor - Secretary-Treasurer:

Dr. V.K. Srivastava
Reader,
Department of Geography,
Gorakhpur University,
Gorakhpur-273 001.

1982: The Commission on Geography of Marketing (of the National Association of Geographers, India) has been established at the 4th Indian Geography Congress at Bombay University (November 1982).
Activities: Since the 4th Indian Geography Congress held at Bombay in November 1982, the annual sessions of the Commission have been organized by the NAGI on the occasion of Indian Geography Congress every year.
Chairman: Prof. L.R. Singh
G.B. Pant Institute of Social Sciences,
80, Tagore Town,
Allahabad - 211 002.

1983: The International Working Group In Market Studies in India

The International Crop Research Institute for the Semi-Arid Tropics (ICRISAT) Patancheru, Hyderabad in coopertion with the Geography Department of Osmania University, Hyderabad, and the International Geographical Union Working Group on Market Place Exchange Systems organized an International Workshop on Agricultural Markets in the Semi-Arid Tropics in October 1983.

One of the recommendations of this Workshop was:

In order to channelize adequately the intellectual interest that has been generated in market studies by this Workshop, it recommends that a 'Working Group in Market Studies' be set up in India with the object of providing a multi-disciplinary forum to pool together intellectual researches available in order (i) to accelerate research on marketing with a view to appreciating its complex problems and processes, (ii) to bring together scholars of varied disciplines to present their research findings; and to emphasize the need of continuing market research as an aid to speeding up the process of economic development.

Thus, for the first time in India, at the international level, it was desired to give rise to an academic body or unit within the International Geographical Union in the sub-field of Marketing Geography to play pivotal role in its progress.

ACADEMIC MEETS

* 1971 Seminar on Market Towns and Spatial Development

National Council of Applied Economic Research/Department of Works, Housing, and Urban Development, Government of India, New Delhi, April 1971 (Organizers).

The Seminar Proceedings have been published by the NCAER in 1972 under the title, Market Towns and Spatial Development.

Papers:

NCAER Background note on development of market towns.

Work Groups

- I: The role of market centres in the development process.
- II: Towns as levers of industrial spread and role of industrial estates.
- III: Planning and development of towns - new and existing criteria for selection.

Aherwadkar, L.J. Role of regulated marketing in the development of market centres - A case study of Marathawada.

Andrade, C.P. and Johnson, A.A. The role of market centres and regulated marketing in the development process - The Khanna example.

Bawa, R.L. *et al.* Market towns and spatial development - A case study of north Bihar.

Bedekar, S.L. Role of regulated markets in the development of rural areas.

Bhat, L.S. Regional planning in India - A suggested model.

Bhawmik, K.L. and Chaudhury, K.K. Rural markets and system of mass communication.

Bose, A.N. Socio-economic basis of small town development.

Bumb, B.L. Regulated marketing in Udaipur district - A case study of Udaipur Mandi.

Garg, P.K. Reorientation of policy for the development of market towns.

Garg, P.K. Small township: A perspective for development.
Gupta, V.K. The system of cities and towns in relation to economic development in India.
Hashim, S.R. Town size and functions.
Johnson, E.A.J. The integration of agrarian, commercial and industrial activities in functional economic areas.
Joseph, S.E. Industrial dispersal in India.
Kahlon, S.S. and Kehal, H.S. Market towns in Punjab and their impact on rural development.
Khan, W. Market centres in Chevella taluk - A descriptive analysis.
Lahiri, T.B. Development of townships - Policies and problems.
Mahalanobis, J.N. Development of townships - Policies and problems.
Maikap, A.K. Role of market centres in Indian economic development with special reference to West Bengal.
Mathai, P.M. Growth Centres.
Mathur, G.C. Innovations in building for speedier development of towns of economical cost.
Muthiah, C. Role of regulated markets in the development process - A case study for Tamil Nadu.
Rao, P.P. and Rao, T.R. Criteria for selection of market towns in India.
Reddy, N.V. Market towns and spatial development in India - A case study of Rayalseema.
Sarkar, A.K. Role of market centres and regulated marketing in the development process.
Selvam, L.G. Planning and development of market towns.
Shah, S.M. Pilot research project in growth centres.
Singh, A.J. Location of regulated markets in Punjab.
Suri, K.B. Growth of small towns in India - A comparative study of rapidly growing and declining towns.
Talwar, B.R. Market towns in Punjab.
Vepa, R.K. Small towns as levers of industrial growth in rural areas.
Vishwanath, M.S. Establishment and development of rurban centres.
Warrior, S.K. Some problems of a public marketing agency and their impact on the marketing development programme.

* 1979 The Third Indo-British Geography Seminar

It was held at Madras, Tirupati, and Mysore in December 1979. The following three papers were directly centered on marketing system and market place trade on the one hand while a good number of papers touched briefly on marketing issues on the other. The topics of marketing problems and rural growth centre strategies were discussed at length. One of the special feature of the seminar was a visit to the Mysore regulated market where inquiries were conducted into regulated markets and their benefits to small farmers. Noteworthy papers are given below.

Papers:

Harriss, B. State intervention in dryland foodgrains markets and price inequality in Andhra Pradesh and Karnataka States.

Jayashanker, D.C. Marketing as a catalyst for regional development - A case study of Karnataka.

Wanmali, S. The regulated and periodic systems of marketing of agricultural produce and their impact on rural development.

* 1980 Workshop on Rural Market Centre Development Programme – Asian Regional Evaluation, Bangalore, FAO/DSE, 1980

Noteworthy Papers:

Mittendorf, H.J. Planning for rural market centre development programme.

Singh, L.R. Spatial aspects of periodic markets and regulated market systems in India - A case study.

* 1981-82 National Workshop on Regulation and Management of Agricultural Produce Markets was organized by the Directorate of Marketing and Inspection at Ranchi (April, 1981), Faridabad, New Delhi, and Pune (May, 1982).

* 1982 International Conference on Improving Geographical Accessibility of Rural Services.
Indian Institute of Management, Bangalore (July 1982).

Noteworthy Paper:

Wanmali, S. *et al.* Equity and efficiency effect of market access for farmers in two regions of India.

* 1983 Symposium on Impact of Weekly Markets on Rural Societies Madurai Kamraj University, Madurai (October 7-10, 1983).

Papers:

Arunachalam, B. The geography of rural markets in India: An inventory and prospects.

Chandran, K. Consumer and traders' attendance and their movement pattern in weekly markets - A case study in Shivganga taluk.

Chandran, K. and Swaminathan, E. Distributional and locational characteristics of weekly market centres - A case study of Shivganga taluk weekly market.

Jamuna, K. *et al.* An understanding towards the locational characteristics, functional organization and trade area of Allinagaram weekly market, Madurai district.

Jothimai, P. and Swaminathan, E. An analysis of functional morphology and the movement of traders, farmers and buyers - A case study on Udumalpet weekly market.

Krishnamurthy, B. A study on weekly cattle market centre: Madurai Thursday cattle market - A case study.

Krishnan, G. Functional classification of weekly markets in South India.

Kumaran, T.V. Market cooperatives and marketing in the Kolli Hills.

Murugesan, N. and Swaminathan, E. Functional morphology and the movement of traders and consumers - A case study of Pudan sandai weekly market, Nammakkal taluk.

Nageswari, S. *et al.* An analysis of spatial distribution of weekly markets in Tamil Nadu State.

Ramaswamy, G. and Sivamurthy, A. Market place participants - A case study of Acharapakkam weekly market.

Rao, M.S. and Kannan, M. Location characteristics and distribution of weekly markets in Ramanathapuram district, Tamil Nadu.

Shantha Kumari, A. Trichy district - A study on locational characteristics and rural weekly markets.

Sivamurthy, A. and Ramaswamy, G. The structure of Acharapakkam weekly market.

Subbiah, S. Ecological complex and evolution of periodic market places in Tamil Nadu - A case study from Tiruchirapalli district.

Swaminathan, E. A study on the locational characteristics of weekly markets in Madurai district.

Swaminathan, E. A comparative study of weekly markets in Coimbatore and Madurai districts in Tamil Nadu.

Velaynathan, S. Rural weekly markets and spatial interaction pattern of consumers in Madurai metropolitan area.

* 1983 International Workshop on Agricultural Markets in the Semi-Arid Tropics, Hyderabad (October, 1983)

The International Crop Research Institute for the Semi-Arid Tropics (ICRISAT) Patancheru, Hyderabad in cooperation with the Geography Department of the Osmania University, Hyderabad and the International Geographical Union Working Group on Market Places Exchange Systems organized an International Workshop on Agricultural Markets in the Semi-Arid Tropics in the month of October, 1983.

It was made clear in the recommendations that there was great significance and relevance of market studies in India and hence there is an imperative need to undertake intensive multidisciplinary research studies on varied marketing perspectives. It was also emphasized that 'we have inadequate knowledge of market systems in India, the typologies of markets in India, market functions, market behaviour etc.' Consequently, the Workshop recommended that a Working Group in Market Studies be set up in India with the object of providing a multi-disciplinary forum to pool together intellectual resources available. The following papers were presented in the meet:

Papers:
The papers presented in the Workshop have been published in the form of a book entitled "Agricultural Markets in the Semi-Arid Tropics" (1985) by the ICRISAT, Patancheru, Hyderabad. The list of papers contributed by the Indian participants is as follows:

Alam, S.M. *et al.* Periodic markets as growth centres in the rural hinterland of metropolitan, Hyderabad.

Desai, G.M. Market channels and growth of fertilizer use in rain-fed agriculture: Conceptual considerations and experience in India.

Dixit, R.S. Spatial organization of market centres in the umland of a metropolis, Kanpur - A case study.

Gopi, K.N. and Dunkerley, J. Fuelwood markets in Hyderabad.

Harriss, B. Agricultural markets and inter-sectoral resource transfers of south-east India.

Jodha, N.S. Market forces and erosion of common property resources.

Menon, K.P.A. Market channels and farmers access to improved seed for rainfed agriculture.

Murthy, K.N. and Oppen von, M. Nutrients distribution and consumer preferences in India - Some policy implications.

Nadkarni, M.V. The role of agricultural markets and market policy - not conducive to rural welfare?

Oppen von, M. *et al.* Impact of market access on agricultural productivity in India.

Raju, V.T. and Bhatt, B.D. Efficiency in pricing and operation of markets for the semi-arid tropical crops in India - A case of groundnut in Gujarat.

Rao, H.S.S. and Maheswari, A. Whither central whole-sale markets?

Rao, K.V.S. *et al.* Impact of market access on agricultural productivity in India.

Rao, P.P. Marketing of fodder in rural and urban areas of India.

Rao, T.V.S. and Subramaniyam, E.V.R.S. Interlocking of credit and product markets and its impact on agricultural productivity.

Sikder, B.P. Marketing of fertilizers and other inputs for rain-fed agriculture.

Srivastava, V.K. Behavioural characteristics of market place participants in the Tarai Region of U.P.

Subbarao, K. Institutions, infra-structure, and regional variations in India's input delivery system.

Verma, S.C. Public interventions in agricultural markets in India.

Wanmali, S. Network of distribution of goods and services in rural India - Some spatial considerations.

* 1984 National Workshop on Regulation and Management of Agricultural Produce Markets, Jaipur (February 1984)

Paper:

Rao, K.V.S. *et al.* A study on impact of regulated markets and roads on productivity and market arrivals in Andhra Pradesh.

* 1985 Fourth National Workshop on Agricultural Markets, Lucknow (1985)

Paper:

Singh, L.R. Spatial organization and planning of agricultural markets in U.P., India.

* 1985 International Conference: Commercial Activities and Rural Development, Gorakhpur University, Gorakhpur (December 23-25; 1985)

The term of the International Geographical Union Working Group on Market Place Exchange System was terminated in August 1984 at the 25th Congress of the IGU in Paris but the General Conference approved the establishment of a new Study Group: Geography of Commercial Activities. Thus, the researches on market place exchange or related forms of trade have to be continued at the international level. In view of this, an international conference was organized in Gorakhpur University on the theme, Commercial Activities and Rural Development, in December 1985.

Papers:

The papers presented in the conference have been published in the form of a book. This publication is under the title, Commercial Activities and Rural Development in South Asia (Srivastava, V.K., 1988, Concept Pub. Co. New Delhi). However , the papers which are directly related to marketing perspectives and/or have been contributed by the Indian participants are as follows:

Bhole, H.G. Mobile trade in rural south India - From the perspective of development theory.

De, N.K. Ecological studies for commercial activities and rural development.

Dixit, R.S. Market centres of a backward economy - Hamirpur district, U.P. (India).

Dubey, R.S. A rational approach to the marketing of foodgrains in M.P.

Gedam, D.A. Sellers' travel behaviour and periodic market cycles in the Wardha Valley.

Hugar, S.I. Periodic non-periodic marketing and rural development in Dharwad District.

Jamkar, A.G. Origin and evolution of periodic market places in Dhule District.

Lal, H. and Yadav, H.R. Development of commercial activities in Gorakhpur city.

Lal, V.N. Commercial activities in a small town - A case study of Bachharawan town in U.P.

Nath, T. and Kushwaha, R.K. The role of market centres in rural development - A case study of Rampur Karkhana block.

Nath, V. and Nath, T. An analytical survey of consumer-trader behaviour in Avadh Plain.

Rao, P.P. and Verhagen, H.M.W.J. Marketing channels of commercial farm inputs in semi-arid tropical India.
Saxena, H.M. Rural market place exchange system in Rajasthan.
Sharma, N. Reorganizing commercial complexes - A core mechanism of rural growth process.
Sharma, S.C. Spatio-temporal changes in the cultivation of commercial crops in Tarai tract of eastern U.P.
Shukla, S.K. Role of commercial activities in the process of rural development - A case study of Sagar region.
Singh D.K. and Routray, R.K. Rural market potential as a measure in regional development.
Sinha, B.R.K. Human resources utilization in commercial activities in rural area - A case study of Dhanaura Block, district Patna.
Srivastava, H.O. The nature of market area regions in Saryupar Plain.
Srivastava, R.C. Marketing systems and problems in the Patha area of Bundelkhand, U.P.
Srivastava, V.K. Geography of commercial activities - A trend report.
Swaminathan, E. Market centres and their hierarchy in Coimbatore region, Tamil Nadu.
Tamaskar, B.G. Economic functions of weekly market places.
Tiwari, R.C. and Lal, N. Spatial planning of rural market centres in Rae-Bareli district U.P.
Twade, M.D. and Gophane, B.N. Marketing organization and commercial fruit farming - The case of Konkan.

CONCLUSION: THE WORK HYPOTHESIZED

The dimensions and trend of the progress of research work in marketing geography in India considered in the aforesaid discussion yield the results shown in Table 11.

The statistics provided in the Table make it crystal clear that during the various periods mentioned, the progress of marketing geography from every stand-point has been considerable in comparison to any previous period excepting, of course, item No. 3 i.e. dissertations. For the 1970s, the number of dissertations, however, is 14 while for the 1980s, it is 8. This is because many works which are near completion have been treated in the discussion as 'in progress' and/or not 'completed'. The number of doctoral dissertations in progress at this time is, actually, more than two and a half dozens. In view of this, it would not be unfair to understand that a considerable amount of knowledge is going to be added to this sub-field of geography during the present decade only.

TABLE 11: DIMENSIONS AND TREND OF PROGRESS IN RESEARCH IN MARKETING GEOGRAPHY IN INDIA

Particulars	*Before 1960*	*1960s*	*1970s*	*1980s*
Research Books/Monographs by Indian Scholars* (1+40)	5	3	15	17
Books/Monographs: Others on Indian Perspectives (29)	1	1	9	18
Research Project Reports - Dissertations (29)	2	5	14	8
Research Project Reports - Other than Dissertations (12)		2	3	7
Research Articles by Indian Scholars (398)	24	33	127	214
Research Articles - Others on Indian Perspectives (27)	4	2	9	12
Total (1+535)	36	46	177	276

* One book undated.

Although a good volume of knowledge was added to the sub-field during the 1960s, nevertheless, it is rightly remarked that marketing geography made a start in taking shape as a separate sub-field only during this decade in the country. In the international context, the studies in this area started, basically, from 1954. Only fragmented studies were made on marketing perspectives within the sphere of geography in India earlier to the 1960s. It has been observed that earlier to the 1960s, there were only 36 studies in all as against 46 during the 1960s, 177 during the 1970s, and 276 during the 1980s (till now).

The number of studies during the 1960s is considerably small (46) as compared to the last decade (i.e. 1970s) and the present (i.e. 1980s) decade (i.e. 177 and 276 studies respectively). Further, in every case, i.e. research books/monographs, research project reports, and research articles (including both full papers, and abstracts), the number for the 1960s is much more small than the corresponding number for the 1970s. Also in every case the number for the 1980s is considerably larger than that during the 1970s.

The geography scholars in the country have shown keen interest in carrying researches on various perspectives of marketing in India. It is a good sign that the number of both the researchers and the researches has been considerably increasing during the past five years.

Besides, in several Indian universities, marketing geography has been included in the syllabi of the postgraduate courses as a special paper. In the various national and international conferences in India, research papers are specifically invited for discussion under the section/session scheduled for marketing geography.

An organization (at the national/international level) named the 'Association of Marketing Geographers of India' has come into being. It brings out a research journal also entitled "The Indian Journal of Marketing Geography"

To promote research work in this sub-field of geography, a Commission, named, Geography of Marketing has come into existence. In addition, national/international conferences, symposia, seminars, workshops on Geography of Marketing have also been held in the country during the recent past.

Thus, there are sound bases to understand that, by this time, in India, Marketing Geography has achieved the status of a branch of its parent discipline, Geography. Within the present framework, therefore, it is safely remarked that, basically, the formative stage has been achieved by Geography of Marketing in the country and with continued research work, its literature is being enriched constantly. Marketing Geography, thus, is passing through the informative stage while the conformative and the reformative stages, a matter of constant multi-dimensional work and process, are, rather, far-ahead.

SOURCE OF INFORMATION

The following are the major sources of information used in the making of the present work:

ICSSR: A Survey of Research in Geography, 3 Vols.
(1972, 1979, 1984).
Journal of Reviews and Abstracts-Geography,
10 Vols. (1975-1984).
Research Projects (1969-1987).
Marketing in Terms of Geography - A Bibliography.

IGU: Newsletters, Working Group on Market Place
Exchange Systems, 15 Vols. (1-15)
Study Group/Commission: Geography of Commerical
Activities, 5 Vols. (1-5).

NCAER: Two Volumes on Market Towns (1965, 1972).

Sinha, B.N.: Progress of Geographical Research
in India, 2 Vols. (1983, 1984).
Recent Trends in Geographical Research in India (1986),
Bhubaneswar, Indian Council of Geographers.

The Indian Journal of Marketing Geography, 4 Vols. (1983-1986).

The works cited in the present work under:

The Reviews and Bibliographies,
Prospective Perspectives.

INDICES

AUTHOR INDEX

SUBJECT INDEX